P9-DCI-153

Recipes from

HISTORIC
HOTELS *of*
AMERICA

 National Trust for Historic Preservation

The Preservation Press

The Preservation Press
National Trust for Historic Preservation
1785 Massachusetts Avenue, N.W.
Washington, D.C. 20036

The National Trust for Historic Preservation is the only private, nonprofit organization chartered by Congress to encourage public participation in the preservation of sites, buildings and objects significant in American history and culture. Support is provided by membership dues, endowment funds, contributions and grants from federal agencies, including the U.S. Department of the Interior, under provisions of the National Historic Preservation Act of 1966. For information about membership, write to the Trust at the above address.

Copyright© 1991, National Trust for Historic Preservation in the United States. All rights reserved. No part of this book may be reproduced in any manner without written permission from the publisher, except for brief quotations used in reviews.

Printed in the United States of America

Library of Congress Cataloging-in-Publication Data

Recipes from historic hotels of America / National Trust for Historic
    Preservation, the Preservation Press ; [compiled and edited by
    David B. Wolinski with the assistance of Suzanne P. Guiry].
        p.   cm.
    Includes index.
    ISBN 0-89133-163-8 : $29.95
    1. Cookery, American. 2. Hotels, taverns, etc. —United States-
    -History. I. Wolinski, David B. II. Guiry, Suzanne P.
    III. Preservation Press.
TX715.R31216 1991
641.5973—dc20   91-10336

Recipes from Historic Hotels of America
was created for The Preservation Press
by Catling *&* Company, Baltimore, Md.

CATLING *&* COMPANY
Executive Editor: Susan J. George
Chairman: Timothy D. Skene Catling
Editor: David B. Wolinski
Text Research: Suzanne P. Guiry
Art Director: Elizabeth Church Mitchell
Type: William C. Bowie

Printed by the John D. Lucas Printing Company, Baltimore, Md.

The producers and publishers of this book make no claims to the authenticity, originality or source of recipes or text submitted by the participants or their representatives.

Introduction

One of life's great pleasures is enjoying a wonderful meal in a beautiful, historic setting. It can sometimes create a memory that lasts a lifetime. It is the expectation of such an experience that makes me appreciate this handsome new cookbook, *Recipes from Historic Hotels of America.*

In 1989, the National Trust for Historic Preservation in Washington, D.C., established Historic Hotels of America, a program that recognizes hotels of historic architecture and ambience in this country. Each member must be at least fifty years old, listed in (or eligible for) the National Register of Historic Places, or be recognized locally as having historic significance. Member hotels are found across the United States. Some are rustic, others are refined. Some are in the country, others in big cities. All are noteworthy for their contributions to our national heritage. What better way to help preserve them and their traditions than with their most favored recipes?

Each hotel's first and featured recipe is complemented by notes—and a beautiful color photo—highlighting its place in the hotel's or region's history. What we learn along the way! A recipe for Indian pudding that is still being made to this day found its origins as a gift to the settlers from the Indians themselves. In the late 1800s, the food was so fine at one Minnesota hotel that the railroad changed its schedules to allow passengers to eat in the hotel's dining room. That restaurant still serves those dishes today, including the featured Bread Pudding with Brandy Sauce. Serendipitously, you will also find out how the pomegranate came to Arizona and about the controversy surrounding a legendary sandwich called The Hot Brown—an argument that has lasted decades and does not seem to be nearly over yet.

And there is more. In these pages we are reminded again of the wonders and wealth of indigenous American cooking, with recipes not only for that Indian pudding, but for gingerbread and spoon bread, chowder, soft-shelled crabs, she-crab soup, apple pie, Key lime pie and pecan pie. Southwestern cuisine, at its most authentic, is featured in a hotel in New Mexico. On Nantucket, a shore dinner replete with scallops, bluefish, tuna and mussels from surrounding waters is being prepared today as it has been for a hundred years. From coast to coast, from the Gulf to the Canadian border, this cookbook honors good food in historic settings. And the color photographs, each taken on location, serve both to further whet the appetite and to encourage us to travel there.

What we have, then, in *Recipes from Historic Hotels of America,* is the best of all possible worlds: memorable destinations, excellent recipes, historical information and traditions that are uniquely American. This book helps preserve the heritage of these historic hotels, and, in doing so, is a treasure itself.

Richard B. Barthelmes
Publisher
Gourmet Magazine

Table of Contents

Welcome

TO HISTORIC HOTELS OF AMERICA

We are pleased to introduce you to Historic Hotels of America,™ a program of the National Trust for Historic Preservation.

The distinguished hotels featured in this book have accepted our invitation to join an exclusive association—one based on historical character, architectural quality and the outstanding preservation efforts made by owners and managers who are dedicated to maintaining each hotel's historic integrity.

We have taken care to select hotels that represent a vast cross section of American traveling experiences. Each offers unique accommodations in one-of-a-kind settings, ranging from rustic to refined, in locales as diverse as mountain wilderness, manicured countrysides, the centers of small towns and bustling metropolises. Though highly diverse, these hotels share a common denominator—an historic environment to enhance your leisure or business trip, coupled with guest services and food and beverage offerings recognized for their outstanding quality.

We invite you to enjoy the hospitality of these fine hotels during your travels. When you do, a portion of your room cost will become a contribution to the National Trust, thus supporting our efforts to preserve America's heritage.

J. Jackson Walter
President
National Trust for Historic Preservation

For information, contact:
Historic Hotels of America
National Trust for Historic Preservation
1785 Massachusetts Avenue, N.W.
Washington, D.C. 20036
202-673-4000

The Adolphus

T he Adolphus is to Dallas what the Parthenon is to Athens ... the tower to London. Well, give or take a few years ...." *Dallas Times Herald.* The famous beer stein turret and symbolic brass eagles and hops on a hallmark chandelier link this remarkable 1912 hotel with its creator, beer baron Adolphus Busch. The hotel's expression of fortune and flamboyance has led critics to name it "the most beautiful building west of Venice." The Beaux Arts hotel, restored in 1981 at a cost of more than $80 million, features a detailed 19-story facade of tapestry brick, granite and slate below a spectacular mansard roof. Exquisite rococo detailing, hardwood paneling, marble and fine antiques grace the renowned interiors.

OVEN-ROASTED BLACK BUCK ANTELOPE
served on a bed of Red Onion Marmalade
Serves 2

Texas Black Buck Antelope, harvested on the Broken Arrow Ranch in Ingram, Texas, has quickly become the meat of choice in the hotel's fine French Room restaurant. Not only does the meat taste mild and sweet, but it also has ⅓ less calories than beef.

Marinate the cut of antelope in wine with carrot, onion, garlic and parsley for 24 hours.

Preheat oven to 350°.

Remove antelope from marinade. In heavy gauge saute pan, heat butter or oil and sear the meat completely on all sides. Transfer to a roasting pan and roast to desired internal temperature (115° to 120° for medium rare, about 20 minutes).

Slice and serve.

Photo, plate 1

Oven-Roasted Antelope

1 12-ounce center-cut black buck antelope loin*, free of fat and sinew

2 cups red wine

1 medium carrot, large diced

1 small onion, large diced

2 cloves garlic, crushed

4 sprigs parsley

2 tablespoons clarified butter or salad oil

* Should antelope be difficult to obtain, venison loin or beef tenderloin are acceptable substitutes.

Red Onion Marmalade

*2 medium red onions, large
 diced*
2 tablespoons butter
1 tablespoon brown sugar
1 tablespoon grenadine

RED ONION MARMALADE

Serves 2

In a heavy stainless saucepan, saute onions in butter until golden brown. Stir in the brown sugar and grenadine just before onions are finished; set aside.

Whipped Potatoes

*2 large potatoes, peeled,
 large diced*
Water to cover
4 tablespoons butter
¼ cup heavy cream, scalded
Salt and pepper to taste

WHIPPED POTATOES

Serves 2

Place potatoes in saucepan and just cover with water. Bring to a rapid boil and cook until fork-tender (20 to 25 minutes).

Drain the potatoes, cool for a few moments; mash well while adding balance of ingredients.

Editor's note: Savory Whipped Potatoes add variety to everyday meals. Experiment with the addition of a generous pinch of your favorite finely chopped fresh herbs or replace the recipe's salt with seasoned salt while mashing to impart a distinctive flavor.

Texas Corn Chowder

Prepare the stock:
*Kernels cut from 6 ears
 fresh corn, cobs reserved*
1 onion, rough chopped
*1 green bell pepper, rough
 chopped*
1 tablespoon butter
1 sprig thyme
1 sprig parsley
3 quarts chicken stock
To finish:
10 strips bacon, diced
1 onion, diced
1 red bell pepper, diced
Kernels from 6 ears fresh corn
3 tablespoons flour
1 cup heavy cream
Salt and white pepper
Fresh thyme
1 cup cooked wild rice
1 cup smoked chicken, diced

TEXAS CORN CHOWDER

8 servings

Gently saute corn and cobs, onion and pepper in butter over medium heat for 5 minutes. Add thyme, parsley and chicken stock. Simmer until liquid reduces by ⅓; strain, reserve stock.

To finish, cook bacon until crisp and remove from pan. Remove all but 3 tablespoons of the drippings; add onion, pepper and corn, saute for 3 minutes. Add flour to make a roux, cook 3 minutes over medium heat.

Add corn stock, stirring constantly. Simmer over low heat for 30 minutes. Add heavy cream and cooked bacon, season with salt, pepper and thyme. Garnish with wild rice and smoked chicken.

MULTI-GRAIN ROLLS
Yield, 16 rolls

Mix all dry ingredients in small mixing bowl with dough hook for 30 seconds. Add all liquids and mix for 2 minutes, until dough pulls cleanly away from sides of bowl; if not, add a touch more flour.

Place dough on floured work surface. Use a rolling pin to roll out the dough to 1-inch thick. Cut into desired shape; allow to rise in a warm place until 1½ times larger than original size.

Preheat oven to 350°.

Place rolls on a floured cookie sheet and bake for 8 to 10 minutes. Brush rolls with Honey Glaze immediately after baking.

GRILLED VEGETABLE KABOBS
Yield, flexible

Having selected your favorite vegetables, clean and prepare them in bite-sized pieces that are easily skewered (firm vegetables such as carrots and mushrooms may require par-boiling before use, to avoid breaking).

Sear over hot flame until tender to the bite.

Editor's note: Although grilled vegetables are delicious served plain, you might enjoy them lightly basted with oil or your favorite vinaigrette just prior to removing from the heat.

Multi-Grain Rolls
1¾ cups bread flour
2 tablespoons cornmeal
2 tablespoons oatmeal
1½ tablespoons semolina
¼ cup rye flour
¼ cup cracked wheat
½ cup malt flakes
2½ teaspoons salt
⅓ cup brown sugar
2 tablespoons plus 2½ teaspoons
* instant yeast*
¾ cup water
¼ cup vegetable oil
1 tablespoon honey
2½ teaspoons molasses
Honey Glaze
⅓ cup honey mixed with
½ cup water

Grilled Vegetable Kabobs
Approximately ¾ cup raw
* vegetables of choice, per serving*

The American Club

KOHLER, WISCONSIN

Photo, plate 2

American Club Smokehouse Salad

For each serving:

6-ounce Kohler Purelean™ Beef
  tenderloin mignon

Peanut oil

Salt and pepper to taste

1 teaspoon each:
  fresh rosemary, basil and
  thyme, or use herbs of your
  preference

Seasonal Greens

Tomatoes for garnish, peeled
  and quartered

Spears of Belgian endive
  (3 per person)

Leaf spinach, stemmed
  and washed

Hearts of Boston lettuce

Oakleaf lettuce

Fresh chanterelles, sliced

Yellow Tomato Vinaigrette

Blend together:

1 cup olive oil

⅓ cup rice wine vinegar

¼ cup shallots, peeled and
  chopped

½ cup yellow tomatoes, diced

1 clove garlic, finely chopped

1 tablespoon brown sugar

Chopped fresh herbs (such as
  basil, thyme, chives, parsley)
  to taste

Salt and pepper to taste

Walter J. Kohler, himself the son of an immigrant, dedicated The American Club in June, 1918 as housing for immigrant laborers—"single men of modest means"—who came to work at the Kohler Company. His goal: that its high standards of living and emphasis on patriotism would instill in the men a love for America. After three years of detailed restoration, the landmark Tudor-style hotel reopened in 1981. True to the spirit of the original American Club, public areas and oak-paneled hallways display antiques and photos of the area's earlier days. Showcasing state-of-the-art Kohler baths, each guest room is different, and honors a famous American with a portrait and framed papers of memorabilia.

AMERICAN CLUB SMOKEHOUSE SALAD
pan-grilled fillet of Kohler PureLean™ Beef with Seasonal Greens and Yellow Tomato Vinaigrette

When Kohler Village was designed in the early 1900s—one of the first planned communities in the United States—creation of a surrounding "greenbelt" was integral to the layout. Kohler Farms was set in this band of meadows and forests to preserve and develop the land. Today, Kohler Farms raises a breed of cattle that feed only on natural grasses and grains, yielding a lower calorie, lower fat, naturally lean product. Kohler PureLean™ Beef is the perfect ingredient to make this hearty salad a good choice for health conscious consumers.

Use enough peanut oil to coat the meat. Marinate overnight in salt, pepper and herbs. Preheat a grill pan over range top, or use charcoal grill. Remove the beef from the oil and herbs and shake off excess, grill until done to your preference.

Arrange tomatoes on the serving plate alternately with the endive. In a bowl, toss the remaining greens with the Yellow Tomato Vinaigrette, remove greens and place in center of the garnished plate. Slice the grilled beef on the bias into thin slices and arrange on the greens, serve.

RIVER WILDLIFE PILAF
wild rice and barley bake
Serves 8 to 10

This "Midwestern pilaf" features grains natively grown in Wisconsin. Like much regional cooking, it is born of the land and the culture, in this case exhibiting an Indian influence in the choice of grains. True to its Midwest heritage, it is hearty fare and a good complement to game dishes. At River Wildlife Lodge in Kohler, this dish is often served with pheasant, duck or seafood entrees.

Preheat oven to 350°.

Saute green onions, peppers, bok choy/celery and garlic in butter on medium heat for 5 minutes. Set aside.

Bake wild rice in the beef stock for 1¼ hours. Saute long grain rice and barley in ½ cup butter until lightly browned. Bake with the chicken stock for 1 hour.

Stir all ingredients together, including parsley, seasonings and optional ¼ cup butter; serve.

River Wildlife Pilaf
1 bunch green onions, diced
1 small red pepper, diced
1 small green pepper, diced
3 stalks bok choy, diced, and/or
3 stalks celery, diced
2 cloves garlic, finely minced
1 cup wild rice
2½ cups beef stock
1 cup long grain rice
1 cup barley
½ cup butter
4 cups chicken stock
¼ cup parsley, finely minced
1 teaspoon seasoned salt
½ teaspoon black pepper
¼ cup butter (optional)

AUTUMN HOMESTEAD VEGETABLES
autumn vegetable gratin
Serves 8 to 10

Austrian, German and Dutch pioneers founded many southeastern Wisconsin towns in the area surrounding the American Club. As these different nationalities met in the new land, recipes would evolve blending traces of each culture. This hearty dish combines favorite vegetables of autumn, many of which could be stored well into winter by the early settlers. With the growing dairy industry, cheese makers were in abundance in the state, creating delectable varieties of cheeses which became flavorful additions to many recipes.

This is a very delicious vegetable dish to accompany hearty entrees such as roast loin of pork, grilled venison steaks or roast duck.

Combine chicken stock and garlic, simmer 15 minutes on low heat. Add cream and heat to just below simmer. Add roux and stir until thickened. Add cheeses and seasonings; cook for 10 minutes, whisking constantly.

Preheat oven to 350°.

Mix all vegetables together, season lightly with salt and pepper. Layer alternately with sauce in 9 x 13-inch pan. Bake uncovered for 1½ hours.

Autumn Homestead Vegetables
For the sauce:
4 cups chicken stock
1 teaspoon garlic, finely minced
3 cups heavy cream
½ cup plus 3 tablespoons roux
2½ cups Swiss cheese, shredded
1½ cups fresh parmesan cheese,
* shredded*
½ teaspoon Tabasco
½ teaspoon black pepper
Salt to taste
The vegetables:
2 cups parsnips, sliced
2 cups kohlrabi, sliced
3 cups brussels sprouts, halved
1 cup onions, sliced
4 cups cabbage, chopped
3 cups potatoes, sliced
Salt and pepper to taste

The American Club

Kettle Morraine Nut Pie

Kettle Morraine Nut Pie

1 cup white sugar

1 cup dark corn syrup

4 eggs

3 tablespoons cornstarch

3 tablespoons butter, melted

½ cup almonds, sliced

½ cup pecan halves

½ cup walnut halves

KETTLE MORRAINE NUT PIE
Yield, 1 9-inch pie

The northern-European immigrants who settled in southeastern Wisconsin brought with them a variety of cooking and baking traditions and styles. The use of nut meats in dessert preparations was popular—nuts provided good flavor and nutrition and avoided spoilage through winter. Even in the state that was to lead the nation in dairy production, homemade ice cream was a treat for early settlers. During summer months, fresh fruit would be added to this chilled delicacy, but in winter various spices were blended into the creamy mixture for tantalizing flavor.

Preheat oven to 350°.

Mix together the sugar, syrup, eggs, and cornstarch until smooth. Add the melted butter, stir until incorporated. Blend in the nuts with half the mixture and fill unbaked pie shell. Use the remaining syrup mixture to fill the pie shell to the top. Bake 45 to 55 minutes.

Remove from oven, cool to room temperature. Serve topped with a scoop of Bourbon Cinnamon Ice Cream.

Basic Pie Crust

3 cups flour

Dash salt

2 cups shortening

1 cup water

1 teaspoon vinegar

BASIC PIE CRUST
Yield, 2 9-inch pie shells

Place flour and salt in bowl. Cut in shortening until it resembles the size of small peas. Add the water and vinegar and incorporate into dough, do not over mix. Divide dough in half, cover with waxed paper and refrigerate for 1 hour to allow dough to relax. Dust lightly with flour, roll to desired size and place in pie pans.

Bourbon Cinnamon Ice Cream

1 quart heavy cream

1⅓ cups sugar

10 egg yolks

4 tablespoons ground cinnamon

2 tablespoons vanilla extract

5 ounces (½ cup plus 2 tablespoons) bourbon

BOURBON CINNAMON ICE CREAM
Yield, approximately 1 quart

Heat the cream and sugar to the boiling point. In a separate bowl, blend the yolks, cinnamon, vanilla and bourbon.

Slowly incorporate a small portion of the heated cream and sugar into the yolk mixture to raise its temperature. Combine yolk mixture with remaining heavy cream. Whip until slightly thick.

Chill the yolk and cream mixture until cool and place in an ice cream machine. Finish according to the machine's directions.

Arizona Inn

TUCSON, ARIZONA

Created in 1930 by Mrs. Isabella Greenway, a dynamic community leader and Arizona's only congresswoman (1933-36), the Arizona Inn was designed to offer friends and guests a sophisticated desert retreat. At its inception the hotel employed disabled servicemen as furniture craftsmen, and provided a market for their work. The adobe-style inn sprawls over 14 acres of landscaped grounds and gardens surrounded by vine covered walls ... a center-city oasis. Still owned and operated by the Greenway family, the inn features many of its original furnishings and artworks—including George Catlin lithographs, Audubon prints and African art acquired on safari—all from Mrs. Greenway's collection.

SHRIMP MAURICE
*butterflied Guaymas shrimp on a bed
of Saffron Rice, with Pomegranate Salsa*
Serves 4

In the days of the early Spanish settlers, seafood was regarded as a delicacy in the Arizona desert. Today, large succulent shrimp fished from the Sea of Cortez are flown regularly from Mexico to Tucson, where local inhabitants still love all forms of fresh fish and seafood. The pomegranate salsa is a variation of traditional Mexican accompaniments, and mixes pomegranate seeds, oranges and cilantro, all harvested from Arizona Inn gardens and grounds.

The pomegranate's native habitat is Africa and eastern Asia. Arizona Inn's Chef, Robertson Reid, named this dish in honor of his Scottish grandfather, Maurice, who pioneered in raising the pomegranate locally.

Wash and clean shrimp. Mix all other ingredients; marinate shrimp for 4 hours.

Place shrimp on skewers, broil for 12 minutes or bake at 375° for 14 minutes. Serve shrimp on Saffron Rice accompanied by Pomegranate Salsa.

Photo, plate 3
Shrimp Maurice
1½ pounds jumbo shrimp, peeled, deveined, tails remaining
½ bunch cilantro
2 cloves garlic, crushed
2 oranges, juiced
2 lemons, juiced
2 limes, juiced
¼ cup olive oil
1 teaspoon salt
¼ teaspoon white pepper

Pomegranate Salsa

2 tangerines, peeled and
  sectioned (reserve juice)
4 pomegranates, peeled, seeds
  reserved
1 small red onion, finely diced
1 bunch cilantro, chopped
1 bunch green onions, diced
1 clove garlic, crushed
1 Serrano (a small, hot pepper),
  finely chopped
1 teaspoon sugar
2 limes
Salt

POMEGRANATE SALSA
Yield, about 1½ cups

Mix all ingredients. The salsa may be served warmed or chilled.

Grilled Tomatillos with Lime Butter

8 medium tomatillos
1 cup butter
1 bunch cilantro, chopped
2 limes, juiced
Salt
Cilantro leaves and
Lime wedges for garnish

GRILLED TOMATILLOS WITH LIME BUTTER
*zesty tomatillos grilled with cilantro and lime butter,
presented on a bed of Red Chile Puree*

Serves 4

Cut tops off tomatillos and sprinkle them with salt. Place face down on a prepared charcoal broiler.

As soon as distinct grill marks are present, turn tomatillos face up and baste with a mixture of butter, cilantro and lime juice. Continue cooking until soft, remove from fire.

Cover bottom of small plate with Red Chile Puree, spread to edges. Place grilled tomatillos on the puree, garnish with cilantro leaves and lime wedges.

Red Chile Puree

½ pound dried red chiles
Water to cover
1 bunch cilantro
6 cloves garlic
2 tablespoons cumin
Salt

RED CHILE PUREE
*this spicy puree may be made well in advance,
and refrigerated*

Serves 4

Soak chiles overnight in enough water to cover. Place chiles in blender or food processor with 2 tablespoons of the soaking water, plus cilantro, garlic and cumin; blend until relatively smooth. Salt to taste.

SAFFRON RICE

Serves 4 to 6

Preheat oven to 350°.

Saute onion and rice in melted butter until rice is well mixed. Add chicken stock and a healthy sprinkle of saffron, bring just to a boil; add bay leaf and cloves. Cover and cook for 18 minutes. When cooled, transfer to serving pan.

Saffron Rice
4 tablespoons butter
½ medium onion, chopped
2 cups Basmati (white rice)
1 quart chicken stock
Spanish saffron
1 bay leaf
2 whole cloves

ROASTED PIÑON SALAD

roasted pine nut salad with Enoki mushrooms

Serves 4

Mix garlic, orange and lemon juice, and olive oil; toss with watercress and red onion; add pine nuts.

Pre-dress plates with red romaine; place the salad on the romaine, garnish with red pepper slices and mushrooms.

Season to taste.

Roasted Piñon Salad
For dressing:
2 cloves garlic, crushed
1 orange, juiced
1 lemon, juiced
½ cup olive oil
2 bunches watercress
1 red onion, sliced
1 cup pine nuts, oven roasted
Salad:
2 heads baby red romaine
1 red pepper, sliced
1 pack whole Enoki mushrooms,
*   cleaned*
Salt
Fresh ground black pepper

SORBET MEDLEY IN A FLORENTINE BASKET

Serves 4

Combine butter, milk, sugar and honey in a medium saucepan, bring to a full rolling boil, stirring occasionally. Remove from heat, stir in almonds and flour until fully incorporated.

Preheat oven to 350°.

Grease and flour a sheet pan. Drop mixture by 4 small ladlefuls at least 6 inches apart on the pan; spread batter into 6-inch circles. Bake for 8 to 10 minutes or until edges are lightly browned and the Florentine is wafer-thin.

Cool for about 1 minute; while pliable, form baskets over an inverted soup cup and cool thoroughly.

At moment of service, scoop in sorbet and garnish with mint leaf.

Sorbet Medley in a Florentine
Basket
6 tablespoons butter
* or margarine*
⅓ cup milk
¼ cup sugar
2 tablespoons honey
1 cup almonds
¼ cup all-purpose flour
1 pint each raspberry, tequila,
* lime and tangerine sorbets, or*
* flavors of your choice*
Mint leaves

Arizona Inn

Blennerhassett Hotel

PARKERSBURG, WEST VIRGINIA

On May 6, 1889 a refined Blennerhassett opened to a boisterous Parkersburg—new laws banned the galloping of horses through town; the hotel's large mirror was guarded by steel against errant gunshots—but its collection of 50 finely appointed rooms, the presence of a First National Bank in its lobby and its popularity with businessmen involved in oil deals made the hotel the centerpiece of the city's move toward sophistication. Modernized in 1944, the hotel, listed in the National Register, enjoyed expansion and detailed renovation in 1986. Particularly notable is its extensive collection of antiques and authentic architectural elements gleaned from period buildings nationwide.

Photo, plate 4

Praline Tulipe

½ cup plus 2 tablespoons butter
1 cup brown sugar
½ cup plus 2 tablespoons
 corn syrup
2¼ cups pecans
1 cup white sugar
1½ cups all-purpose flour
10 scoops praline ice cream
1¼ cups chocolate sauce
Whipped cream
20 whole strawberries
10 whole chocolate wafers
Sprigs of mint

PRALINE TULIPE
Serves 10

In its original form, praline (attributed to the cook of Marshal Duplessis-Praslin, 1598-1675) became a crumbly candy creation popular with the Creoles. This has evolved into our crunchy, flower-shaped "tulipe" filled with old-fashioned praline ice cream, chocolate sauce and wild, wonderful, West Virginia strawberries. It is truly a grand finale to any meal and has assumed regal status as the signature dessert of the historic Blennerhassett Hotel.

Melt butter in saucepan. Add brown sugar, corn syrup, pecans, white sugar and flour, 1 at a time, stirring well before each addition. Cook over low heat for 12 minutes, stirring to avoid scorching.

Preheat oven to 325°.

Cover 2 sheet pans with buttered waxed paper. Place 5 scoops of the mixture on each sheet pan, with the dollops spaced equally to allow for spreading. Bake for 15 minutes or until golden brown. Remove from oven, cool for 1 minute, then remove each portion and place over an upside-down soup cup. Praline shell will set in about 3 minutes.

Place shell in the center of a dinner plate. Scoop praline ice cream into the shell. Ladle chocolate sauce over the ice cream, garnish with whipped cream, strawberries, chocolate wafer and a sprig of mint.

Carl Edwards Photography

COLOR PLATE 1
Oven-Roasted Black Buck Antelope, page 1
The Adolphus, Dallas, Texas

Photography: Image Studios

COLOR PLATE 2
American Club Smokehouse Salad, page 4
The American Club, Kohler, Wisconsin

Balfour Walker Photography, Inc.

COLOR PLATE 3
Shrimp Maurice, page 7
Arizona Inn, Tucson, Arizona

Photography: Richard Alabaugh & Lawrence Demme

COLOR PLATE 4
Praline Tulipe, page 10
Blennerhassett Hotel, Parkersburg, West Virginia

COLOR PLATE 5
Roast Veal Loin Prince Orloff, page 13
The Broadmoor, Colorado Springs, Colorado

Photography: John Nation

COLOR PLATE 6
Herbed Rack of Kentucky Spring Lamb, page 16
The Brown — A Camberley Hotel, Louisville, Kentucky

Photography: Barry Meriash

COLOR PLATE 7
Chicken Mousseline, page 19
The Brown Palace Hotel, Denver, Colorado

Photography: Eric Roth

COLOR PLATE 8
Marinated Salmon with Caviar, page 22
The Copley Plaza Hotel, Boston, Massachusetts

LEMON CHICKEN
Serves 6

Trim the chicken breasts of any fat, season each piece with salt and pepper, set aside.

Combine flours and baking powder in a bowl. Beat the egg with the water, and quickly incorporate into the flour.

In a double boiler (or a mixing bowl over boiling water) combine the marmalade and lemonade to make a sauce, mixing until smooth.

Heat the oil to 375° in a shallow frying pan. Dip the chicken in the batter and place in the oil. Reduce the heat to 325°, continue frying, turning frequently for 2 to 3 minutes, or until golden brown.

Pour the heated citrus sauce over the breasts, serve at once.

Lemon Chicken
6 boneless, skinless chicken
  breasts
Salt and pepper
2 to 3 cups vegetable oil,
  for frying
For batter:
1 cup self-rising flour
½ cup chestnut flour
  (or cornstarch)
½ teaspoon baking powder
1 egg
1⅓ cups water
½ cup sweet orange marmalade
½ cup frozen lemonade
  concentrate

STRAWBERRIES ROMANOFF
Serves 6

Wash strawberries, remove stems; place in bowl with Grand Marnier, sugar, orange rinds and melba sauce. Toss a few moments to blend, cover, refrigerate for 1 hour.

Remove from refrigerator, incorporate whipped cream; add ice cream and stir just enough to blend. Divide mixture into individual sherbet glasses or dessert dishes, serve.

Strawberries Romanoff
1 quart fresh strawberries
½ cup Grand Marnier
4 tablespoons sugar
2 orange rinds, grated
2 tablespoons melba sauce
  (page 125)
2 cups heavy cream, lightly
  sweetened, whipped stiff
4 scoops vanilla ice cream,
  softened

Blennerhassett Hotel

Soft-Shell Crabs
Oil for deep frying
8 large soft-shell crabs, cleaned
Old Bay seasoning
1 clove garlic, minced
1 cup flour
1 egg, slightly beaten with
1 cup milk
2 cups bread crumbs
Choron Sauce
1 cup Creole Sauce (page 121)
1¼ cups Béarnaise Sauce
  (page 119)

SOFT-SHELL CRABS
with Sauce Choron
Serves 8

Heat deep-frying oil to 350°.

Season crabs with Old Bay and minced garlic, dust with flour; dip in egg/milk mixture, then in bread crumbs.

Using tongs, deep fry crabs for 3 minutes or until golden brown; drain on paper towels. Place on serving plates, spoon with Choron Sauce, serve immediately.

For Choron Sauce fold the cooled Creole Sauce into the fresh Béarnaise Sauce. Serve immediately.

Planked Salmon
2¾ to 3 pounds salmon, pin
  bones and skin removed
1 seasoned pine plank
Marinade
½ cup Grey Poupon Country
  Style mustard
¼ cup dry white wine
¼ cup extra virgin olive oil
1 tablespoon garlic, finely
  minced
1 tablespoon fresh ground pepper
2 tablespoons fresh chives,
  chopped
2 tablespoons fresh tarragon,
  chopped
1 tablespoon fresh parsley
1 tablespoon green onions, thinly
  sliced
1 teaspoon salt
½ cup raw bacon, minced
Mustard Raifort Sauce
Combine in a small bowl:
1 cup mayonnaise
1½ teaspoons Dijon mustard
1 tablespoon fresh lemon juice
2 tablespoons fresh horseradish
½ cup sour cream

PLANKED SALMON
with Mustard Raifort Sauce
Serves 10 to 12

Preheat oven to 450°.

Mix all marinade ingredients (except salt and bacon) until smooth. Use pastry brush to spread evenly over both sides of salmon to create a thick coating. Season with salt, scatter half the bacon over the plank where the salmon will rest, position salmon, sprinkle with balance of bacon.

Place plank on flat baking sheet, bake for 25 minutes; remove, cool to room temperature.

Serve salmon on the plank, with Raifort Sauce.

SEASONING A PINE PLANK

Purchase a natural pine plank (check to be sure it is natural pine, not fire-proofed or water-proofed) 18- to 24-inches long, at least 9-inches wide, and 1-inch thick. (Measure your oven first to ensure fit.)

Rub ¼ cup vegetable oil onto both sides of the plank. Place on oven rack and bake or "season" at 325° for 5 hours. The board will give off some smoke and an odor similar to that of wood being sawed. Baking the plank burns off tar and resins from the wood, imparting a nutty, roasted aroma to foods cooked on it. Once a board is seasoned, it may be reused.

The Broadmoor

COLORADO SPRINGS, COLORADO

Consisting of pale pink buildings with red tile roofs and set on the edge of a lake, this perfect mountain resort has been called the "Riviera of the Rockies." The three separate hotels that constitute this landmark are anchored by the traditional eight-story Broadmoor Main, built in the Italian Renaissance style in 1918. Developed by Spencer Penrose, a prospector who made millions in copper and gold mining, and designed as both "permanent and perfect," continuous expansion programs have added new components virtually every year to the sprawling 3,000-acre resort.

ROAST VEAL LOIN PRINCE ORLOFF
Serves 16 to 18

During the 18th and 19th centuries, members of the Russian aristocracy spent entire seasons—and sometimes years—in France. Many of the Russians were highly respected gourmets, and the Parisian chefs would name dishes in their honor. Orloff (also Orlov) is the name given to a traditional method of preparing loin of veal, named for the Russian Prince Orloff. The following method of preparation for rack of veal, while popular in Europe—and exquisite—is not common in the United States. However, it is often served at The Broadmoor, where it has been a favorite for decades.

Preheat oven to 370°.

Trim fat from back of veal rack leaving just a thin layer on top, continue trimming on both sides of loin. Place the saddle right-side-up, use a knife point to prick the large sinew all the way down the spine to avoid contraction during cooking. Slice fat into thin layers; use fat to entirely cover the veal loin, secure with string.

Place veal loin in roasting pan, season with salt and pepper. Roast uncovered for 1½ hours. Plunge an instant-reading meat thermometer into thickest part of meat, wait 45 seconds for a reading (internal temperature should reach 115° to 120° for medium rare). Remove from oven, allow to rest 30 minutes before carving.

Create a decorative rosette with prepared Rice Soubise. Serve au jus.

Photo, plate 5
Veal Loin
1   15- to 17-pound rack of veal
Salt and pepper
Rice Soubise (page 14)

Rice Soubise
4 tablespoons butter
2 pounds onions, finely minced
12 ounces rice
2 cups chicken stock
6 tablespoons butter
Salt and pepper
Nutmeg

RICE SOUBISE

Preheat oven to 325°.

Saute onions in 4 tablespoons butter for 3 minutes. Add rice and chicken stock, cover and cook in oven for 45 minutes or until thoroughly cooked. Using grinder or food processor, grind entire mixture. Add 6 tablespoons butter, salt, pepper and nutmeg to taste. Use a pastry bag to create a rosette garnish.

Mushroom and Herb Cheese
Strudel

2 tablespoons butter
1 teaspoon shallots, chopped
¼ teaspoon garlic, minced
¼ teaspoon fresh thyme,
  chopped
¼ teaspoon fresh rosemary,
  chopped
1 cup shiitaki mushrooms, sliced
½ cup chanterelle mushrooms,
  sliced
½ cup button mushrooms, sliced
¼ cup sherry
½ cup brown sauce (page 119)
¼ cup herbed boursin cheese
3 sheets phyllo dough (from your
  grocer's freezer)
Melted butter, for brushing

MUSHROOM AND HERB CHEESE STRUDEL
Serves 4

Preheat oven to 375°.

Melt butter in saute pan, saute shallots, garlic and herbs for a few moments; add mushrooms, saute 2 to 3 minutes more. Add sherry, mix in brown sauce, cook 3 more minutes, remove from heat. Blend in boursin cheese.

Brush thawed phyllo sheet with butter, top with next sheet, brush with butter, top with last sheet. Spread Strudel mixture evenly across one end of dough, roll up dough and place on baking sheet. Brush finished roll with butter; bake for 10 to 12 minutes.

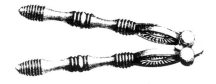

Grand Marnier Souffle
3 tablespoons butter
3 tablespoons flour
3 tablespoons sugar
¾ cup milk
4 egg yolks, beaten
1 tablespoon orange zest
4 egg whites
2 tablespoons Grand Marnier
3 tablespoons sugar

GRAND MARNIER SOUFFLE
Serves 4

Preheat oven to 400°.

In saucepan, heat butter until melted. Add flour and sugar, cook until incorporated, about 4 to 5 minutes. Add milk, egg yolks and orange zest, cook 3 more minutes, remove and cool.

Whip egg whites to stiff peaks. Add Grand Marnier to saucepan mixture, fold in egg whites.

Lightly butter a ceramic souffle dish, coat with sugar, tap out excess. Fill dish to top with souffle mix. Bake in water bath for 35 to 40 minutes. Serve immediately.

STUFFED PHEASANT BROADMOOR

Serves 4

Preheat oven to 475°.

Bone the pheasant breasts. Fold back the breast fillet and flatten the breast with a mallet. Lightly season the breasts with seasonings. Place 2 tablespoons Mushroom Duxelle onto each breast and wrap the breast around it; wrap each rolled breast in a blanched cabbage leaf. Cut pork fat into 4 equal sections, wrapping each one around one of the cabbage-covered breasts (or wrap each in sliced bacon).

Place breasts on a baking sheet and bake for 8 to 10 minutes. Do not overcook ... pheasant tends to dry easily.

To serve, ladle 3 to 4 tablespoons Pheasant Sauce on each serving plate. Slice wrapped pheasant breast at a 30 to 35° angle; fan into a ¾ circle, arrange Green Grapes Caramel in the opening.

MUSHROOM DUXELLE

Yield, 1 cup

In a saute pan, heat olive oil; add shallots, garlic and mushrooms, cook until all liquid is evaporated. Add parsley, season with salt and pepper; mix in glace de viande and reduce slowly until a spreadable mix is achieved.

NATURAL PHEASANT SAUCE

Preheat oven to 450°.

Coarse-chop carcasses and legs. Heat bacon fat or oil in a heavy roasting pan in the oven, add carcasses and legs and brown evenly. Add carrots, celery and onion; braise. Add seasonings, mixing well (do not burn). Add cold water so the bones are well covered. Bring to a boil, lower heat to a very low simmer, simmer covered for about 12 hours.

Strain stock through a fine mesh strainer into a saucepan, reduce by boiling until ¾ cup remains. Mix cornstarch with sherry and brandy, whisk into the boiling stock, remove from heat, strain.

Stuffed Pheasant Broadmoor

2 pheasants, 2- to 2¼-pounds each
Salt, pepper, garlic powder, cinnamon, ground rosemary and ground thyme, for seasoning
½ cup Mushroom Duxelle
4 large leaves Savoy cabbage, blanched
½ pound pork caul fat (pork netting) or 8 thin slices bacon
1 cup Natural Pheasant Sauce
Green Grapes Caramel (page 124)

Mushroom Duxelle

¼ cup olive oil
¼ cup shallots, chopped
1 tablespoon garlic, chopped
½ pound fresh button mushrooms, finely chopped
Pinch parsley, chopped
Salt and white pepper
½ cup glace de viande

Natural Pheasant Sauce
For stock:
2 pheasant carcasses (bones), including the legs
½ cup bacon fat or cooking oil
2 carrots, course cut
2 stalks celery, course cut
1 large onion, finely chopped
Pinch parsley
½ teaspoon each dried rosemary and thyme
Salt, to season
4 bay leaves
1 tablespoon cracked black peppercorns
To finish:
2 tablespoons cornstarch
2 tablespoons each sherry and brandy

The Brown—A Camberley Hotel

LOUISVILLE, KENTUCKY

Fourth and Broadway, Louisville's "Magic Corner," has been home to the Brown since October 25, 1923. On that date, the Brown was overflowing with a congratulating public, who for years made the hotel a city landmark. Yet, as a victim of the malaise affecting many urban centers, the hotel suffered growing indignity until its renaissance beginning in 1979, which brought this Southern landmark back to its original grandeur. Highlights include intricate plaster molding, detailed woodworking, stained glass and original crystal chandeliers. A phenomenal restoration and revitalized destination in the heart of the city, this architectural masterpiece is indeed worth a special visit.

Photo, plate 6
Herbed Rack of Kentucky Spring Lamb
1 8-bone (about 1½ pound) rack of lamb
4 teaspoons olive oil
½ teaspoon dry oregano
½ teaspoon dry thyme
Salt
Course ground black pepper
1 clove garlic, crushed
2 cups beef stock or bouillon

HERBED RACK OF KENTUCKY SPRING LAMB
Serves 4

A long-time product of Kentucky, spring lamb has been a favorite entree at The Brown Hotel's English Grill restaurant for many years. Enhanced by select herbs, the delicate flavor of locally grown lamb is as much a tradition to The English Grill as the Derby is to Kentucky. The Brown tradition is today, as it was at its opening in 1923, one of welcoming hospitality and fine cuisine.

Cut all fat from bones about 3½ inches down. Rub meat with some olive oil; rub in herbs, salt, pepper and garlic. Heat remaining olive oil in medium roasting pan, sear meat in oil on all sides, discard oil.

Preheat oven to 350°.

Add beef stock to pan, roast for 25 minutes (medium rare); 35 minutes (medium).

Remove lamb from pan and reduce stock until thickened. Place knife along side of bones and follow down to end. Place bones on plate and place meat on top of bones; strain sauce and pour over meat.

Fried Oysters in Cream and Lemon Dill

Serves 2

Toss oysters in flour, then in egg, then bread crumbs. Saute oysters in ½ of butter until browned, set aside; discard oil.

To pan, add cream, salt and pepper to taste and remaining butter. Stir until thickened. Finish with dill and lemon juice.

Pour sauce onto plates and set oysters on top. Garnish with dill sprig.

Salmon in Herbed Lemon Cream

Serves 4

Heat oil in pan. Flour fillets and saute until brown on both sides. Discard oil. Return to heat and add wine, herbs, lemon, salt and pepper to taste. Cover and reduce over low heat by ⅔. Add cream and reduce by ½.

Remove fillets. Finish sauce with butter. Reduce until thickened. Pour sauce over fillets.

Kentucky Limestone Salad

Serves 2 to 3

Wash and dry lettuce, cut bottom off of head. Shingle all leaves around plate. Crumble bleu cheese on top, toss pecans over top and garnish with red pepper strips.

Serve with Creamy Raspberry or Raspberry Vinaigrette dressing.

Fried Oysters in Cream and Lemon Dill
8 large fresh oysters, shucked
½ cup flour
2 eggs, lightly beaten
1 cup bread crumbs
½ stick butter
¾ cup heavy cream
Salt and pepper
1 teaspoon fresh dill, chopped
2 tablespoons fresh lemon juice

Salmon in Herbed Lemon Cream
¼ cup olive oil
½ cup flour
4 6-ounce salmon fillets
¾ cup white wine
1 teaspoon dry basil
1 teaspoon dry oregano
½ teaspoon fresh lemon
Salt and pepper
¾ cup heavy cream
4 tablespoons butter

Kentucky Limestone Salad
1 head Kentucky limestone lettuce (bibb lettuce may be substituted)
1 ounce bleu cheese
¼ cup roasted pecans
1 red pepper, cut in strips

The Brown

Creamy Raspberry Dressing
½ cup sour cream
¼ cup raspberry vinegar
⅓ cup sugar
3 tablespoons melba sauce
 (page 125)

Raspberry Vinaigrette
¾ cup melba sauce (page 125)
¾ cup tarragon vinegar
3 tablespoons sugar
1 clove garlic, minced
⅓ cup olive oil
Salt and pepper to taste

The Hot Brown
½ cup butter
Flour (6 to 8 tablespoons)
 to make a roux
3 to 3½ cups milk
6 tablespoons grated parmesan
 cheese
1 egg, beaten
2 tablespoons whipped cream
 (optional)*
Salt and pepper
8 to 12 slices of bread, toasted
 (may be trimmed)
Slices of roast turkey
Extra parmesan cheese for
 topping
8 to 12 strips fried bacon
Cling peaches, for garnish*
*The debate rages over whipped
 cream in the sauce and whether
 or not peaches complemented
 the original presentation. It
 now seems a—albeit tasty—
 matter of choice.

CREAMY RASPBERRY DRESSING
Serves 4

Place sour cream in mixing bowl. Whisk in vinegar, sugar and melba sauce. Chill 1 hour before serving.

RASPBERRY VINAIGRETTE
Yield, about 2 cups

Place melba sauce in a mixing bowl. Whisking slowly, add vinegar, sugar, garlic, oil, salt and pepper.

THE HOT BROWN
Serves 4 to 6

"The Hot Brown was developed three or four years after the hotel opened when the supper dance business was falling off. The band would play from 10 until 1 and when they took a break around midnight people would order food. It was ham and eggs, so we decided we needed something new. The Chef (Fred K. Schmidt) said, 'I have an idea for an open-faced turkey sandwich with Mornay sauce over it.' I said, 'That sounds a little flat,' so the chef said, 'I'm going to put it under the broiler.' The maitre d' said, 'It should have a little color, too." So Schmidt said, 'We'll put two strips of bacon on top of it.' I said, 'How about some pimento.' And that's how The Hot Brown came to be."

Rudy Suck, Hotel Manager.

"Lunchtime favorite was always The Hot Brown. Maybe 200 people would be eating lunch and 190 of them would be eating Hot Brown sandwiches."

Fred Caldwell, Head Waiter

Quotes from *The Brown Hotel and Louisville's Magic Corner*, 1984, Broadway Project Corporation.

In saucepan, melt butter and add flour to make a roux. Add milk and parmesan cheese; thicken sauce with the egg (do not boil), remove from heat. Fold in whipped cream; salt and pepper to taste.

For each serving, place 2 slices of toast on a metal or heat-proof dish, cover toast liberally with turkey. Pour a generous amount of sauce over the turkey, sprinkle with additional parmesan. Place dish under broiler until sauce is brown-speckled and bubbly, remove from broiler. Cross 2 pieces of bacon on top, sprinkle with parmesan, serve immediately.

The Brown Palace

DENVER, COLORADO

In the late 1800s, respected businessman Henry Cordes Brown, owner of a triangular lot at the intersection of 17th and Broadway, retained architect Frank E. Edbrooke to design an "unprecedented" hotel in the popular Italian Renaissance style. Featuring the now famous eight-story, stained glass atrium lobby, and hailed as the second fireproof building in America, construction finishes included granite from the Colorado Rockies, sandstone from Arizona and fine onyx from Mexico. After four years of construction at a cost of $1.6 million, a remarkable expenditure for the time, The Brown Palace opened in 1892.

CHICKEN MOUSSELINE
with Tomato Fennel Cream Sauce
a torta of panfried pignoli-crusted chicken mousseline in striped pasta on a creamy sauce of roast garlic, sun-dried tomatoes and fennel
Serves 12

Pasta originated centuries ago in the Orient and was brought to Europe by Marco Polo. Although the basic recipe for pasta is timeless, creating new ways to serve it provides endless creative challenges.

At The Brown Palace Hotel's award-winning restaurant, Palace Arms, Chef Dan Groen and his colleagues set culinary trends by focusing their creativity on upscale food preparation and presentation. The following recipe is just one example of their answer to a basic chicken and pasta dish.

Saute onion and garlic in butter until tender, place in bowl, chill.

Pass chicken meat through smallest die of a chilled meat grinder. Process chicken, anchovies and sauteed onions and garlic in food processor until smooth, then slowly add eggs and cream. Add peppercorns and process briefly into small pieces.

Scrape mixture into a stainless bowl, set bowl on ice and fold in remaining ingredients, except breading. Between sheets of plastic wrap, roll out Mousseline to ½ inch thick. Cut into 24 equally sized triangles.

Combine parsley, pine nuts and bread crumbs, sprinkle breading mixture over meat and press in lightly, refrigerate.

Photo, plate 7
Chicken Mousseline
½ yellow onion, minced
1 teaspoon garlic, ground
2 tablespoons clarified butter
2 pounds uncooked chicken meat from fryer chicken
8 to 10 anchovy fillets
2 whole eggs
1½ cups heavy cream
1½ tablespoons green peppercorns
2 tablespoons fresh chervil leaves, chopped
1 teaspoon nutmeg
1 teaspoon white pepper
Breading:
2 tablespoons parsley, chopped
2 tablespoons pine nuts (pignoli), chopped
2 tablespoons coarse bread crumbs
(Continued, page 20)

To serve:
Oil, for frying
Pasta
Tomato Fennel Cream Sauce
Diced tomato, for garnish
Fennel leaves, for garnish

Tomato Fennel Cream Sauce
¼ cup olive oil
1 head fennel, 1-inch julienne
  (reserve tops for garnish)
½ medium yellow onion,
  1-inch julienne
½ cup dry white wine
2 cups strong chicken stock
1 quart heavy cream
15 cloves garlic, roasted in skin,
  then peeled
3 ounces prosciutto ham,
  1-inch julienne
2 teaspoons each: chopped fresh
  rosemary, thyme, parsley,
  fennel leaves
1½ teaspoons cayenne pepper
3 to 4 ounces sun-dried
  tomatoes, thinly sliced
¾ cup amaretto

Basic Pasta
2 cups all-purpose flour
1½ cups durum semolina flour
1 whole egg
2 teaspoons salt
½ teaspoon olive oil
¾ cup cold water

Pan fry chicken in hot oil until golden brown and just done, do not overcook.

Rewarm pasta in boiling water, drain well.

Ladle 3 ounces (scant ⅓ cup) Tomato Fennel Cream Sauce onto center of plate, spreading to edges. Beginning with pasta, alternately layer 3 pieces of pasta and 2 of chicken. If desired, garnish with diced tomatoes and fennel leaves.

Sun-Dried Tomato, Roast Garlic and Fennel Cream Sauce
Yield, approximately 1½ quarts

Heat olive oil in heavy saucepan, saute fennel and onion, deglaze with wine; add stock and reduce by ½. Add cream and garlic, reduce until thickened; add remaining ingredients, simmer 10 minutes.

Basic Pasta
Serves 12

Using a food processor or pasta maker, mix Basic Pasta ingredients according to the manufacturer's instructions.

Roll out pasta dough into ½-inch thick rectangles, wrap and allow to rest; refrigerate overnight.

On a lightly floured board, cut pasta into ½-inch wide ribbons. Create a "rainbow" by aligning alternate ribbons side by side. Tack together with wet pastry brush; run through a pasta roller to desired thickness.

Cut pasta into 3½-inch by 3½-inch triangles. Cook in boiling salted water for 2 to 2½ minutes; plunge in cold water to stop the cooking, drain and refrigerate. Remaining pasta may be frozen.

Colored pastas
Any one of the following is adequate for 12; producing all recipes creates more than 5 pounds of pasta, enough for 75 servings!

For variations on the basic recipe, add or replace ingredients as follows:

Green (spinach): Replace the ¾ cup water with ¾ cup pureed spinach.

Red (tomato): Replace the ¾ cup water with ¾ cup pureed tomatoes.

Yellow (saffron): Crush 1½ teaspoons saffron threads into ¾ cup hot water and steep for 10 to 15 minutes, chill. Use the liquid to replace the water in the basic recipe. (Turmeric powder may be substituted for the saffron.)

Black (squid ink): Mix 4 packages squid ink (available at most gourmet grocery stores) with enough water to make ¾ cup liquid. Use the liquid to replace the water in the basic recipe.

Smoked Trout in Corn Pudding

Serves 12

tasty smoked Colorado rainbow trout in a steamed corn-pudding wrapper, accompanied by a relish of tomatillos, red onions and mint

Split trout in half lengthwise. Lay on smoker racks, skin side up, hot smoke according to manufacturer's directions for 6 to 8 minutes. Remove fish, cool, peel off skin. Set aside.

In a saucepan over medium heat, saute corn, onion, jalapeño and garlic in butter. Add cream, reduce by ½; add stock and cornmeal, stir frequently for 5 to 6 minutes. Add chopped cilantro, lime juice and baking powder, mix, add eggs. Turn into a casserole dish and refrigerate for 1 hour.

On a piece of plastic wrap (about 12 x 12 inches), use a spatula to spread 2 ounces of the corn mixture in the approximate shape of a fish fillet. Lay 1 fillet on top, skin side down. Cover with 1 layer each of red and green peppers.

Place 1 more fillet on top, skin side up; gently spread with 2 more ounces corn pudding. Fold over the plastic wrap into an envelope shape, tucking ends under. Repeat with remaining fillets. Steam over boiling water for about 15 minutes, until corn is semi-firm to the touch.

Leaving plastic wrap in place, use a sharp knife to slice warm trout into 6 even pieces. Remove plastic wrap; place 3 pieces on each serving plate with 1 tomatillo (see recipe below), lid replaced. Extra relish may be served on the side. Garnish with cilantro.

Note: This dish is also nicely accompanied by sour cream.

Smoked Trout in Corn Pudding
6 8-ounce boneless rainbow trout
4 ears fresh corn, kernels removed
⅓ yellow onion, minced
2 jalapeño peppers, seeded, minced
1 teaspoon fresh garlic, minced
3 tablespoons butter
1½ cups heavy cream
1 cup chicken stock
2 cups yellow cornmeal
½ bunch cilantro, chopped
Juice of 1 lime
3 teaspoons baking powder
4 eggs
4 red bell peppers, roasted, peeled, seeded and sliced
4 Anaheim (mild green) chilies, roasted, peeled, seeded and sliced
Cilantro for garnish

Tomatillo, Red Onion and Mint Relish

Serves 12

Pull husks back from tomatillos, do not remove completely. Slice off top of tomatillo (including husk), reserve for garnish.

Use a melon baller to remove meat of tomatillos, dice small. Combine with balance of ingredients. Refill the tomatillos with the mixture; reserve extra.

Tomatillo, Red Onion and Mint Relish
12 large tomatillos
1 large red onion, small diced
4 tablespoons mint, chopped
¼ cup honey
Juice of 1 lemon
Salt and pepper

The Brown Palace

The Copley Plaza Hotel

BOSTON, MASSACHUSETTS

Designed by Henry J. Hardenbergh, architect of New York's Plaza Hotel, the Copley Plaza opened August 19, 1912. Built on the original site of the Museum of Fine Arts, the hotel quickly became a landmark on Copley Square in Boston's Back Bay. Exquisite, ornate architectural detail is common, having been painstakingly restored in renovations begun in 1973. Accommodations feature period antiques, each rare and distinctive. Of particular note is the Venetian Room, resplendent with gold leaf and baroque detail. These luxurious features have earned the hotel the nickname "Grande Dame of Boston."

Photo, plate 8

Marinated Salmon

1 whole side of fresh salmon

10 ounces sea salt

1 onion, minced

3 carrots, minced

1 cup celery, minced

¼ cup olive oil

⅓ cup fresh dill, chopped

Vinaigrette

(prepare just prior to serving)

⅓ cup shallots, chopped

⅓ cup parsley, chopped

¼ cup champagne vinegar

¾ cup olive oil

Dash salt and pepper

For garnish:

4 ounces Beluga caviar or
  Golden Ossetra

Fresh chervil

MARINATED SALMON WITH CAVIAR
Serves 12

The Scandinavian custom, particularly prevalent in Sweden, of having a marinated salmon appetizer and a glass of aquavit before a meal dates back countless years. Each a quintessential favorite of the gourmet palate, this fine combination of North Atlantic Salmon and fine Beluga caviar has been a perennial favorite of Copley Plaza guests.

Cover the salmon with the sea salt and marinate for 24 hours. Wash and dry and cover for the next 24 hours with the minced vegetables. Wash and dry and marinate for 24 hours with the olive oil and chopped dill.

Slice the salmon very thinly and divide on 12 plates. Bask with the Vinaigrette and garnish with caviar and fresh chervil. Serve with Potato Pancakes or Blini.

POTATO PANCAKES
Serves 6

Wash and peel potatoes, cover with cold water, let stand for 2 or more hours, drain and rinse. Grate potatoes with a fine grater, squeeze out excess liquid. Add onion to potatoes; quickly mix in flour, egg, salt, pepper and soda.

Heat 1 tablespoon butter in a large skillet. Add 1 spoonful of the mixture for each pancake, spreading with the spoon to make them as thin as possible. Cook gently until lightly browned on the bottom, turn and brown the other side. Add more butter to the skillet as needed, continue until all the mixture is used. Serve immediately.

Potato Pancakes
6 medium potatoes
1 medium onion, finely chopped
1 tablespoon flour
1 egg, lightly beaten
¾ teaspoon salt
¼ teaspoon white pepper
½ teaspoon baking soda
Butter, for frying

BLINI
Yield, 36 to 40 blini

Scald milk, cool to lukewarm; mix in yeast. Add sugar and ½ of the flour, mix well. Cover and sit in a pan of warm water until batter doubles in bulk (about 1 hour and 15 minutes).

Blend egg yolks with butter and salt, add to batter. Add balance of flour, beat until smooth. Cover, let rise until doubled in bulk (about 30 minutes).

Beat egg whites until stiff, fold into batter, let stand 10 to 15 minutes.

Heat a griddle or large skillet, butter lightly. Spoon batter into skillet, 1 spoonful per blini. Bake until golden brown, turn and finish.

Blini
2 cups milk
1½ teaspoons instant dry yeast
1½ teaspoons sugar
3 cups all-purpose flour, sifted
3 eggs, separated
5 tablespoons butter, melted
½ teaspoon salt
Butter, for cooking

The Copley Plaza Hotel

Veal Tenderloin

12 2-ounce veal tenderloin
  medallions

Salt and pepper

¼ cup butter

1 cup veal stock

¾ cup butter

Fresh tarragon

Pea pods, baby carrots and
  pearl onions, for garnish

Red Wine and Tarragon
Marinade

Blend together:

2 cups red wine

¼ cup shallots, chopped

⅓ cup carrots, chopped

3 tablespoons celery, chopped

3 tablespoons garlic, chopped

1 tablespoon fresh tarragon,
  chopped

Salmon Fillets

4 5- to 6-ounce salmon fillets

¼ cup butter

¼ cup shallots, chopped

⅓ cup white wine

¼ cup dry vermouth

½ cup fish stock

⅓ cup heavy cream

Salt and pepper

Lemon juice

Fresh thyme leaves

½ pound fresh beans
  (fava, black beans, green beans,
  butter beans)

¼ cup butter

VEAL TENDERLOIN
marinated in Red Wine and Tarragon
Serves 6

Place the veal in the marinade for 12 hours.

Season medallions with salt and pepper and saute in butter until pink, keep warm. Add the marinade and reduce by ½. Add the veal stock and reduce by ½, whisk in butter.

Place the veal tenderloins on a plate and cover with sauce. Garnish each medallion with fresh tarragon, garnish the plate with pea pods, baby carrots and pearl onions.

SALMON FILLET WITH A HARVEST OF BEANS
Serves 4

Preheat oven to 350˚.

Lightly season the salmon fillets with salt, saute in butter for a few minutes. Finish in oven (8 to 10 minutes), keep warm.

Gently saute shallots in butter, add wine and vermouth, reduce by ½; add fish stock, reduce by ½. Add cream and reduce until creamy. Season lightly with salt, pepper and a sprinkle of lemon juice.

Quickly saute beans in butter. Place the sauce on serving plates. Press the salmon in the middle and garnish with the beans. Sprinkle with thyme leaves. Serve with rice or boiled potatoes.

El Encanto

E l Encanto—The Enchanted—fittingly describes this unique retreat set on 10 tropically landscaped acres overlooking Santa Barbara and the Pacific Ocean. The original six red-tile-roofed cottages, built in 1916 in an area called the Riviera, were designed as college housing. Later converted, the property opened as a hotel in 1918. Following the addition of 12 Spanish-style bungalows in 1931, the hotel became a posh winter retreat for Hollywood stars and affluent East Coast and Midwestern businessmen. Beginning in 1977, the grounds and the hotel—having grown to 100 rooms and cottages—were completely restored, with guest rooms and public areas richly appointed in a French country style

GARLIC-GRILLED SANTA BARBARA SPOT PRAWNS
Serves 4

Spot prawns are a hidden treasure brought in by local fisherman from Santa Barbara's sparkling Pacific waters. A simple marinade of Santa Barbara extra virgin olive oil, garlic and the hot surface of the grill bring out the prawns' succulent sweetness. A modest salad of cilantro leaves and crisp cucumbers, dressed with the oil and sherry vinegar accompanies the prawns.

Olive oil was an important part of Santa Barbara's past, a product of the many huertos or olive orchards on the hills and in the valleys surrounding the beautiful Santa Barbara mission. The prized Santa Barbara oil was exported to Spain, an important resource of California's colonial days. Today, the rich, fruity flavor of the Santa Barbara olive oil is prized by epicures across the United States.

Peel the shells from the prawns, retaining tails, devein. Marinate the prawns in garlic and olive oil, cover and refrigerate for at least 2 hours, preferably overnight.

Preheat grill to very hot. Season prawns with salt and pepper. Grill quickly on each side, taking care not to overcook. (Prawns are done when they just turn opaque and lose translucency) Place 3 prawns on bed of Cucumber and Cilantro Salad on each plate.

Drizzle remaining olive oil over prawns, garnish with limes.

Photo, plate 9
Garlic Grilled Santa Barbara Spot Prawns
12 jumbo Santa Barbara (10 to a pound) spot prawns*
1 tablespoon garlic, chopped
4 tablespoons Santa Barbara extra virgin olive oil
Salt and fresh ground pepper, to taste
6 tablespoons Santa Barbara extra virgin olive oil
2 limes, halved, for garnish
* or shrimp

*Crisp Cucumber and Cilantro
Salad*

3 tablespoons sherry vinegar
6 tablespoons Santa Barbara
   extra virgin olive oil
Salt and fresh ground pepper,
   to taste
½ medium cucumber, hothouse
   or "European" (seedless)
1 small bunch fresh cilantro

Garlic Mashed Potatoes
12 12-ounce russet potatoes
12 ounces whole garlic cloves,
   peeled
1 cup cream*
¼ of a nutmeg, freshly grated
1 teaspoon salt
Fresh ground black pepper
½ pound unsalted butter*
*For special non-dairy or low-
   cholesterol diets, the cream may
   be replaced with non-fat milk
   and the butter with extra
   virgin olive oil.

CRISP CUCUMBER AND CILANTRO SALAD
Serves 4

In small bowl, mix vinegar and olive oil; season with salt and pepper. Slice cucumber in thin rounds. Pluck the individual leaves of cilantro and toss with the cucumbers and dressing. Divide the salad into 4 portions and place on center of each plate.

GARLIC MASHED POTATOES
Serves 12

Call it rustic cooking, or just plain old-fashioned home style, this recipe for mashed potatoes with garlic is one of the most requested recipes from the El Encanto Hotel. Don't skimp on the garlic! *While the quantity of fresh garlic cloves may seem terrifying, these potatoes are mild and smooth. Don't substitute chopped garlic; the result is harsh and best avoided. Garlic Mashed Potatoes is a simple dish that is excellent for entertaining. The potatoes can be made ahead and kept warm or reheated at the last minute.*

Peel and quarter the potatoes. Boil the potatoes with the whole peeled garlic. When the potatoes are cooked (about 20 minutes), remove from heat and drain immediately.

Place potatoes in a mixing bowl and whip with a whisk or an electric mixer. Heat the cream, add to the potatoes. Season with nutmeg, salt and pepper to taste. Finish by whisking the butter into the hot potatoes.

EL ENCANTO BOUILLABAISSE

Serves 8

For stock select bones from firm-fleshed fish: halibut, sea bass or snapper (do not use tuna or mackerel bones). In a large heated roasting pan, heat olive oil until smoking hot; add fish bones, brown lightly. Remove to large pot.

Add balance of ingredients, bring to boil, reduce heat and simmer 45 minutes—do no allow to burn. Strain.

Cut fillets into 1-ounce chunks; clean mussels to remove "beards," set aside.

The Soup: heat olive oil in large, heavy bottomed pot; saute fennel, onion, celery and leek until tender. Season with salt and pepper to taste, add thyme, saffron and dried orange peel. When vegetables are translucent, add bouillabaisse stock and simmer 20 minutes; add potato and simmer until cooked.

Add sauvignon blanc, bring to simmer. Add mussels, simmer 2 minutes. Add fish chunks and quickly bring to boil; reduce heat to simmer and cook until fish is just done and flakes when fork-tested. Mussels should be opened by this point—discard any that are not.

Ladle bouillabaisse into large serving bowl or individual bowls, sprinkle with chopped parsley. Spread Rouille on bread or stir into broth as desired.

El Encanto Bouillabaisse
For 2 quarts fish stock:
2 pounds fish bones
¼ cup olive oil
¼ pound sliced fennel
¼ pound onions, sliced
2 stalks celery, sliced
9 cloves garlic, chopped
⅓ bunch thyme
1 bay leaf
1 tablespoon basil, chopped
2 tablespoons tomato paste
1 quart chicken stock
1 quart water or shrimp stock
½ teaspoon cayenne pepper

Bouillabaisse
¼ cup olive oil
7 ounces fennel, julienne
7 ounces onion, julienne
6 ounces celery, julienne
6 ounces leeks, julienne
Salt
Fresh ground pepper
⅓ bunch thyme
2 generous dashes saffron
Dried peel of ¼ orange,
* shredded*
2 quarts fish stock
½ russet potato, peeled
* and thinly sliced*
1 cup sauvignon blanc
1 pound red snapper fillets
1 pound sea bass fillets
1 pound halibut fillets
40 mussels
¼ cup Italian parsley, chopped
16 slices French bread,
* fried in olive oil*
Rouille (page 123)

El Encanto

The Greenbrier

WHITE SULPHUR SPRINGS, WEST VIRGINIA

Throughout the 19th century, The Greenbrier was *the* Southern summer resort. Guests came to use the mineral water, to enjoy the mountain climate and to mingle with the famous of the day. Today many of the original cottages are preserved as guest accommodations, although enlarged and modernized. In 1913, the central Georgian section of The Greenbrier opened on a year-round basis, with golf and tennis as featured attractions. Subsequent additions to this National Historic Landmark have refined the hotel's architecture to reflect the colonial Virginia style. Following use as an army hospital during World War II, the hotel's interior was redecorated by Dorothy Draper.

ROAST CHICKEN BREAST GREENBRIER VALLEY
Serves 8

The nutty, earthy taste of chanterelle mushrooms from West Virginia's Greenbrier Valley are featured in this elegant but easy chicken breast dish.

Use a sharp paring knife to remove the meat from the drumsticks and thighs; discard skin, fat and bone. Puree in food processor; add egg white and process a few seconds more. Transfer the mixture to a metal or glass bowl set in larger bowl of ice (the mixture must stay chilled). Use a wooden spoon to beat the cream into the mixture, a little at a time, making sure the cream is fully incorporated at each stage. Season with a generous pinch of salt and pepper, refrigerate.

Cook shallot in 1 tablespoon butter until soft, but not brown. Add wild mushrooms and saute 3 to 5 minutes over medium heat until all moisture has evaporated. Add minced garlic and madeira and cook until any moisture evaporates, let cool.

Melt 1 tablespoon butter in small saucepan, add spinach, toss until leaves are wilted and liquid is rendered. Remove from pan, squeezing out any remaining liquid between your hands. Chop coarsely, let cool.

Blend chicken mixture, cooled mushroom mixture, cooled spinach mixture, herbs and corn in food processor a few seconds until combined.

Photo, plate 10

Roast Chicken Breast Greenbrier Valley

4 double chicken breasts, skin on, with bone

2 chicken drumsticks, chilled

2 chicken thighs, chilled

1 egg white, chilled

½ cup heavy whipping cream, chilled

Salt and fresh ground black pepper

1 tablespoon shallot or onion, chopped

2 tablespoons butter

¾ cup fresh chanterelles or other wild mushrooms, chopped

1 small clove garlic, minced

(continued, page 29)

Heat oven to 400°.

Slide your finger between the skin and the flesh of the chicken breasts to create a pocket. Spread an equal amount of the filling mixture under the skin of each breast half (a piping bag with plain large tip is easiest). Press down the skin to seal. Brush breasts with melted butter, season with salt and pepper.

Place breasts on baking sheet and roast for 30 minutes, until skin is golden brown and juices run clear when breast is pricked with a skewer. Remove pan from oven, cover loosely with foil and leave in warm place for 5 to 10 minutes to allow juices to redistribute throughout the meat.

When ready to serve, cut or pull each breast half from the bone, then slice into 3 diagonal portions to display the filling. Arrange on warmed plates. Serve with fresh-buttered pasta and a variety of steamed vegetables such as tiny green beans, baby carrots or sliced yellow squash.

1 tablespoon madeira, port or sherry
1 cup loosely packed fresh spinach leaves*, washed, stems removed
1 tablespoon chopped fresh herbs (parsley, chives, tarragon, chervil)
2 tablespoons corn kernels
Melted butter for brushing
*If using frozen spinach, thaw, squeeze out all moisture. Measure out about 2 tablespoons, chop coarsely.

ROASTED GARLIC AND THYME SPOON BREAD
Serves 10

Preheat oven to 375°.

Roast unpeeled garlic until soft, about 10 minutes, peel. Reduce oven temperature to 325°.

Add garlic to milk, bring to boil. Whisk in the cornmeal, pouring in a thin stream to avoid lumps. Reduce heat, continue cooking for 15 minutes, stirring constantly. Consistency should be thick but creamy—if it appears too thin, add more cornmeal after a few minutes.

Remove pan from heat. Beat in egg yolks 1 at a time; stir in butter, add thyme. Season to taste with salt and pepper.

Puree the mixture in food processor until very smooth. As close to cooking time as possible, whip egg whites to a soft peak and carefully fold into the mixture.

Butter 10 4-ounce ramekins and fill ¾ full with the mixture. Bake in water bath covered with a sheet of parchment paper for about 30 minutes. To prepare in larger individual ramekins or 1 large baking dish, simply increase the cooking time slightly.

Roasted Garlic and Thyme Spoon Bread
4 cloves garlic, unpeeled
1 quart milk
2½ cups yellow cornmeal
3 egg yolks
3 tablespoons butter
1 tablespoon fresh thyme, chopped
Salt and white pepper, to taste
3 egg whites

The Greenbrier

Greenbrier Bread Pudding

15 slices white bread
½ cup melted butter
6 whole eggs
1 quart milk
1¼ cups sugar
1 cup raisins
1 teaspoon vanilla extract
Vanilla Sauce

GREENBRIER BREAD PUDDING WITH VANILLA SAUCE
Serves 8 to 10

Preheat oven to 450°.

Cut the bread slices into 1-inch squares and toast lightly in the hot oven. Reduce heat to 350°.

Place the toasted bread in the bottom of a 2½-quart ovenproof dish, drizzle with the melted butter. Combine the remaining ingredients, mix well, pour over the bread.

Bake until the custard is firm, approximately 45 minutes. Serve with Vanilla Sauce.

Vanilla Sauce

2 cups heavy cream
½ cup sugar
4 egg yolks
1 tablespoon all-purpose flour
1 tablespoon vanilla extract
¼ teaspoon salt
2 scoops vanilla ice cream

VANILLA SAUCE
Yield, 1 quart

Combine the cream and sugar in a 2-quart saucepan and bring just to a boil; remove from heat. In a bowl, beat the egg yolks, flour, vanilla and salt. Stir in a little of the hot cream, add this mixture to the rest of the hot cream.

Cook the sauce over low heat, stirring constantly with a wooden spoon until just thickened (do not let the mixture get too hot, or the eggs will curdle). Remove from heat, add the ice cream, stir until melted. Strain the sauce through a fine sieve. The sauce may be served hot or cold.

Chilled Peach Soup

1 quart Greenbrier fresh frozen
  peaches (or canned cling
  peaches), drained
¾ cup sour cream
¾ cup pineapple juice
1 cup orange juice
¼ cup lemon juice
¼ cup dry sherry
½ cup juice from the peaches

CHILLED PEACH SOUP
Serves 8

In a blender, combine the peaches and the sour cream until smooth. Add the remaining ingredients and mix thoroughly. Strain and serve chilled.

Hawthorne Hotel

SALEM, MASSACHUSETTS

In the 1920s, inspired by civic pride, the citizens of Salem established an unusual public subscription drive to build "Salem's own hotel ... to meet the needs of Salem, its guests and visitors ...." The Hawthorne has been a unique and integral part of the city and Boston's North Shore ever since. Beautifully restored, the stately Federal-style hotel is central to the attractions of historic Salem—the Salem Witch Museum, Essex Institute Museum neighborhood, Peabody Museum, House of the Seven Gables, Pickering Wharf, Salem Harbor and numerous notable homes are all within walking distance on the famous Heritage Trail. The Hawthorne is one of only three Massachusetts hotels selected as a "Landmark Lodging Establishment" by the state's travelers' guide.

VEAL HAWTHORNE
fine sauteed veal with lobster and Orange Hollandaise

Serves 4

The signature dish of the hotel's renowned restaurant, Nathaniel's, is an original blend of the freshest ingredients. This creation is named for Nathaniel Hawthorne, famed author of The House of the Seven Gables *and* The Scarlet Letter.

Heat clarified butter in large saute pan. Dredge veal medallions in flour, shake off excess. Saute over medium-high heat for about 45 seconds, turn and saute 20 seconds more.

Add lobster, asparagus and white wine, cover; saute additional 20 to 30 seconds to heat through. Remove from heat, salt and pepper to taste.

To serve, place veal on plate, 2 pieces per person. Top with asparagus spears and ¼ of the lobster. Finish with Orange Hollandaise, serve immediately.

Photo, plate 11
Veal Hawthorne
¼ cup clarified butter
8 veal medallions, 2½ ounces each
Flour for dredging
8 ounces cooked lobster meat, cut in pieces
12 asparagus spears
¼ cup white wine
Salt and pepper
Orange Hollandaise (page 32)

Orange Hollandaise

Orange Hollandaise

1 cup orange juice

4 tablespoons orange marmalade

3 yolks from large eggs

2 teaspoons lemon juice

⅛ teaspoon Tabasco

1¼ cups clarified butter

Salt to taste

ORANGE HOLLANDAISE

Yield, approximately 1½ cups

In a heavy pan, reduce orange juice and marmalade until thick and bubbly (take care not to burn). Reserve at room temperature.

In double boiler or stainless steel mixing bowl over medium saucepan of simmering water, place egg yolks, lemon juice and Tabasco; whisk constantly until mixture appears thick and frothy.

Incorporate clarified butter by adding a few drops at a time, then a thin stream, whisking constantly. When butter is incorporated, stir in the reduced orange mixture. Check taste, adjust with salt and additional lemon juice if necessary.

Oysters Suzanne

4 tablespoons shallots, chopped

4 tablespoons butter

¼ cup dry vermouth

1 bunch Swiss chard, cleaned and chopped

2 tablespoons flour

2 cups heavy cream

Pinch cayenne pepper

3 tablespoons Dijon mustard

Pinch mace

Salt and pepper

16 oysters

¾ cup Swiss cheese, grated

Rock salt

OYSTERS SUZANNE

Serves 4

Rich in flavor and tradition, oysters have been a favorite of New England diners since colonial times. Even the most discriminating palate will relish this culinary creation, an original recipe created by the Hawthorne's Executive Chef, Steve Nelson.

Saute 2 tablespoons shallots in 2 tablespoons butter over low heat until golden. Add vermouth and chard, steam until limp, reserve.

In heavy pan, saute balance of shallots in 2 tablespoons butter over medium heat for 3 minutes. Add flour to make roux, cooking 5 minutes. Add heavy cream, stir until thickened and smooth; simmer a few minutes more. Add cayenne, Dijon mustard and mace, salt and pepper to taste.

Preheat oven to 350°.

Open oysters and disconnect from shell, reserving the best side and discarding the other. Put 2 tablespoons chard mixture in each shell, top with oyster; finish with Dijon cream sauce and sprinkle with grated cheese.

Place oysters on layer of rock salt in ovenproof dish, bake until golden brown and bubbly. Serve immediately.

Creamy Peppercorn Dressing

1 teaspoon minced garlic

2 tablespoons minced onion

3 tablespoons lemon juice

2 cups mayonnaise

2 tablespoons fresh cracked black or butcher's pepper

2 tablespoons grated parmesan cheese

CREAMY PEPPERCORN SALAD DRESSING

Yield, approximately 2¼ cups

a simple yet hearty dressing guaranteed to become one of your favorites

In mixing bowl, blend garlic, onion and lemon juice; add mayonnaise and pepper, mix well; add parmesan cheese, blend.

Hawthorne Lobster Stew

Serves 4

it's best to prepare this delicious stew the night before to allow time for its rich flavors to be revealed

Boil lobsters (page 120); pick meat and tomalley, cut meat into generous pieces.

Saute shallots in butter, add the lobster and tomalley, and cook over low heat for about 3 minutes. Add sherry and continue sauteing for 2 more minutes. Cool for 5 to 10 minutes. Add milk slowly, stirring gently.

Refrigerate overnight (or for a minimum of 5 to 6 hours). Slowly reheat at service time, making sure not to bring to a boil. Serve with fresh ground black pepper.

Hawthorne Lobster Stew
4 1-pound lobsters
1 tablespoon shallots, minced
½ cup unsalted butter
2 tablespoons dry sherry
1 quart milk
Fresh ground pepper to taste

Chicken Dundee

Serves 4

Split the chicken breasts and dredge in flour. Saute in butter on both sides until almost done. Add almonds and scallions and saute briefly; add Scotch, flame to burn off alcohol. Add heavy cream and mustard; simmer to reduce sauce and finish coating the chicken. Season with salt and white pepper to taste.

Place 2 pieces of chicken breast on each serving plate, top with sauce.

Chicken Dundee
4 boneless chicken breasts, skin removed
Flour, for dredging
2 tablespoons butter
4 tablespoons sliced almonds
4 scallions, sliced
¼ cup plus 2 tablespoons (3 ounces) Scotch whiskey
¾ cup heavy cream
3 tablespoons Dijon mustard
Salt and white pepper

Salem Seafood Chowder

Serves 6 to 8

Heat butter, add celery and onions, cook until clear. Add flour, stir well. Reduce heat to low, cook for 15 minutes (taking care not to brown).

Add clam and fish stock and cook ½ hour, stirring frequently.

Add all seafood and cook an additional ½ hour or until seafood is done.

Add cream and potatoes, season with thyme, salt and pepper to taste, bring back up to temperature. Serve immediately.

Salem Seafood Chowder
1 cup butter
½ cup celery, diced
½ cup onions, diced
1 cup flour
1 quart clam stock or clam juice
1 quart fish stock
6 ounces scallops
6 ounces baby shrimp
4 ounces clams, chopped, in juice
6 ounces white fish (cod, scrod, monk, haddock, etc.)
1 quart heavy cream
1 cup potatoes, ½ inch diced, parboiled until just firm
1 teaspoon thyme
Salt and pepper

Hawthorne Hotel

The Hay-Adams Hotel

WASHINGTON, D.C.

At the turn of the century, when John Hay and Henry Adams were paragons, social and political Washington revolved around their adjoining homes on Lafayette Square. When the Hay-Adams Hotel, an Italian Renaissance design by Mirhan Mesrobian, was built on the same site in 1927, it remained the epicenter of polite society. Charles Lindbergh, Amelia Earhart, Sinclair Lewis and Ethel Barrymore were frequent guests. Today, this classic hotel has been restored to its original grandeur, a restoration hailed by *Architectural Digest*. The Hay-Adams ... short of a presidential invitation, as close as one can come to staying at the White House.

MARYLAND CRAB CAKES
on a bed of Fennel Sauce
Yield, 6 cakes

For decades, The Hay-Adams has been Washingtonians' destination for fine dining. A counterpoint to a world of extravagant tastes, guests continue to enjoy many traditional, simple, yet elegant dishes for which the Hay is famous, including this favorite rendition of the ever popular crab cake, synonymous with Maryland and the historic Chesapeake Bay.

Pick through crabmeat to remove shells. Gently mix in diced bread, mayonnaise, eggs, Worcestershire, Old Bay, sauteed peppers and onions and ¼ cup butter. Form into 6 patties, roll in brioche crumbs.

Heat clarified butter in a skillet, cook patties to a golden brown, gently turning just once, making sure crab cakes are heated all the way through. Serve on a bed of Fennel Sauce and decorate with sliced lemon and chopped parsley.

Photo, plate 12
Maryland Crab Cakes
1 pound jumbo lump crabmeat
4 slices white bread (crust removed), diced
1½ cups mayonnaise
2 whole eggs
Worcestershire to taste
Old Bay seasoning to taste
3 tablespoons red bell pepper, lightly sauteed, finely diced
3 tablespoons green onion, lightly sauteed, finely diced
¼ cup butter
1 6-day-old brioche (or croissant or dinner roll), finely diced
1 cup clarified butter
Fennel Sauce (page 35)
Sliced lemon and chopped parsley for garnish

FENNEL SAUCE

Yield, about 1½ cups

Burn off alcohol, add crème fraîche, bring to a boil; add salt, pepper and chopped fennel, stir to an even finish.

Fennel Sauce
¼ cup pernod
1½ cups crème fraîche
  (page 120)
Salt and pepper to taste
¼ cup chopped fennel leaves

PEA SOUP WITH COUNTRY HAM

Serves 6

Reserving 3 to 4 tablespoons of peas for garnish, stew the balance of the peas with the chicken stock, ¼ cup butter, leeks, lettuce leaves, chervil, salt and sugar until cooked.

Process in a blender, then pass through a fine sieve; adjust consistency if needed. Cook the reserved peas in 1 tablespoon butter. Finish the soup at the last moment with the remaining butter; garnish each plate with a few of the reserved peas and diced country ham.

Pea Soup with Country Ham
1½ pounds shelled fresh or
  frozen peas
3 cups chicken stock
½ cup plus 2 tablespoons butter
2 leeks, sliced
1 cup shredded lettuce and sprigs
  of fresh chervil
Salt to taste
Pinch of sugar
⅓ cup cooked country ham,
  diced

DUCK WITH MINT

Serves 4

Season duck and put mint inside. Secure opening, wrap duck in a large piece of white cloth and tie each end. Boil carrot, onion, celery and seasoning in enough water to cover duck. Place duck in liquid. Cover and simmer 2½ hours.

Remove duck from cloth and drain. Surround with mint and serve with Mint Sauce and turnip puree.

Duck with Mint
1 large fresh duck
1 large bunch mint
1 carrot, quartered
1 large onion, stuck with 3 cloves
1 stalk celery
1 garlic clove, crushed,
  for seasoning
Salt and pepper to taste
Mint for garnish

MINT SAUCE

Yield, about 2 cups

Place shallots, herbs, vinegar and wine in a small pan. Season and bring to a boil. Reduce liquid by ⅔, cool.

Whisk in egg yolks and cook on low heat. Whisk in butter bit by bit (do not boil). When sauce thickens, season with lemon juice. Strain into a gravy boat, stir in extra mint. Keep warm.

Mint Sauce
1 tablespoon each shallots and
  chervil, chopped
1 sprig thyme
1 small bay leaf
⅓ cup white wine vinegar
⅓ cup white wine
Salt and pepper to taste
3 large egg yolks
1 cup butter, cut in pieces
  and slightly warmed
1 tablespoon lemon juice
2 tablespoons mint

The Hay-Adams Hotel

Chicken with Mussels

Chicken with Mussels

1 4- to 5-pound roasting chicken
1 large onion, chopped
1 large carrot, chopped
2 to 3 tablespoons olive oil
1 bouquet garni
1 cup dry white wine
*4 to 5 pounds mussels, scrubbed
   and scraped*
Parsley
Salt and pepper to taste

Serves 4 to 6

Brown chicken and vegetables in oil. Transfer to a deep pot. Add bouquet garni and half the wine. Season, cover and cook gently for 45 minutes.

Steam 1½ pounds mussels (discard any dead mussels—those which are cracked or are open—prior to cooking) in remaining wine by cooking over high heat. Discard shells. Reserve liquid. Put mussels in cavity of chicken after cooking. Strain liquid into pot and arrange remaining mussels around chicken. Cover and cook 45 minutes.

Place chicken on serving dish. Arrange mussels in shells around it; garnish with parsley, keep warm. Skim fat from juices, season and boil, strain.

Serve chicken with crisp bread and a tossed salad.

Summer Berry Pudding

Summer Berry Pudding

*2 pounds black currants and
   raspberries or a mixture of red
   currants and blackberries*
1½ cups sugar
White bread, one day old
1 cup whipping cream
Grand Marnier or cherry brandy

Serves 8 to 10

Mix fruit and 1 cup sugar and leave overnight. Next day, bring mixture to a boil and simmer for 1 minute. Strain liquid from fruit and reduce by ⅓. Return ½ the remaining liquid to fruit. Set other ½ aside.

Remove crusts from bread. Cut a circle from 1 slice to fit the base of a 2½-pint pudding mold. Cut wedges to fit around sides. Leave no gaps. Pour in fruit, cover top with a layer of bread. Put a plate on top with a tin as a weight. Leave overnight in the refrigerator.

Turn onto serving dish and pour the remaining liquid over it. Whip cream, ½ cup sugar and brandy. Decorate pudding with rosettes of cream. Serve remaining cream in a gravy boat.

Cobb Salad

Cobb Salad

2 cups romaine lettuce
*¼ chicken breast, poached,
   medium diced*
½ medium tomato, diced
¼ medium avocado, diced
3 strips cooked bacon, chopped
Bleu cheese (optional)

Cobb Dressing
Yield, about 2 cups:
1 egg yolk
⅓ cup white vinegar
1 cup salad oil
½ cup chili sauce
2 tablespoons sugar
¼ cup chopped watercress
Pinch thyme, oregano, basil
2 cloves garlic, minced
Salt and pepper to taste

For each serving:

Make a bed of romaine, top with chicken, tomato, avocado, bacon and bleu cheese.

For dressing, blend egg yolk and vinegar in bowl. Work in salad oil slowly, add chili sauce and remaining ingredients. Use a little water to adjust consistency if needed.

The Heathman Hotel

PORTLAND, OREGON

When The Heathman opened in 1927, it was the toast of Broadway—Portland, Oregon style—with a clientele of entertainment luminaries, lumber barons and railroad magnates. The hotel's elegant past is preserved in its Italian Renaissance facade and in its heart, the eucalyptus paneled Tea Court; both restored to their original glory when the hotel reopened in 1984. Fine antique furnishings blend with contemporary designs. An extensive art collection ranges from 18th-century canvases to Andy Worhol's famed *Endangered Species* series silkscreens, and original art by Northwest artists is found in each of The Heathman's guest rooms. The hotel's meeting rooms and suites are named for the city's many bridges and founding families.

GRILLED MEDALLIONS OF VENISON
with Apricot and Green Peppercorn Glaze
Serves 4

Heathman Chef Greg Higgins established the hotel's reputation for award-winning, Pacific Northwest cuisine. The Heathman Restaurant places prime importance on fresh local products. Northwest fish and game, such as salmon, quail, duck, rabbit and buffalo are popular entrees; Oregon free-range venison, appearing on the menu seasonally, is a symbol of Northwest bounty.

Marinate the venison medallions with the olive oil, fresh herbs and garlic in a shallow dish or plate. Cover with plastic wrap and refrigerate for at least 3 hours (overnight is preferable, if time allows).

In a large saucepan over medium heat, saute the minced garlic and shallots in the olive oil, stirring frequently as the mixture begins to brown (3 to 5 minutes). When evenly golden brown, add the wine, vinegar, peppercorns and apricots. Flame off the alcohol and allow the mixture to reduce slightly. Add the stock and reduce by about ½, or until the sauce will coat a spoon. Lower the heat to warm and season to taste with salt and pepper.

Charcoal-grill or pan-fry the medallions to your preference (3 to 5 minutes per side). Serve on a bed of Apricot-Peppercorn Glaze; accompany with roasted potatoes and fresh herb garnish.

Photo, plate 13

Grilled Venison
1½ pounds boneless venison loin,
  cut in 3-ounce medallions
¼ cup olive oil
2 tablespoons mixed herbs
  (rosemary, thyme, marjoram,
  etc.), finely chopped
6 whole cloves garlic, split in half

Apricot Green Peppercorn Glaze
¼ cup garlic, finely minced
½ cup finely shallots, minced
2 tablespoons olive oil
2 cups marsala wine
¼ cup balsamic vinegar
¼ cup canned green peppercorns
1 cup dried apricots, julienne
2 quarts game stock or mixture
  of chicken and beef stocks
Salt and pepper

Quail with Wild Rice and Roasted Shallots

Quail with Wild Rice and Roasted Shallots

8 boneless whole quail

Salt and pepper

1 teaspoon dried thyme (or 1 tablespoon fresh thyme), finely chopped

4 cups cooked wild rice

8 shallots, peeled and left whole

1 cup dry sherry

½ cup white wine vinegar

1 cup heavy cream

Fresh herbs, for garnish

QUAIL WITH WILD RICE AND ROASTED SHALLOTS
Serves 8

Preheat oven to 425°.

Season the cavities of the quail with a pinch of salt, pepper and thyme. Using a small spoon, fill with wild rice so the quail plump slightly. Place them in a shallow roasting pan with the peeled shallots, taking care that none of the birds touches another. Add the sherry, vinegar and any remaining thyme to the pan. Roast until the birds and the shallots are golden brown (20 to 30 minutes). The quail are ready when a joint is pricked and the juices run pink to clear. Remove birds from the pan and arrange on a serving platter with the shallots.

Pour the pan juices into a small saucepan and reduce by simmering to ¼ the original volume. Add the heavy cream and continue simmering to reduce until the sauce thickens (5 to 10 minutes); season to taste with salt and pepper. Serve the sauce around the birds and shallots on the platter, garnish with fresh herbs.

Szechuan Pepper Broiled Salmon

Szechuan Pepper Broiled Salmon

6 to 8 6-ounce salmon steaks or fillets (1 per serving)

Cilantro Crème Sauce

1 cup white wine

2 cups sour cream

2 tablespoons cilantro, finely chopped

2 tablespoons green peppercorns

4 limes (3 juiced, 1 sliced)

Salt and pepper to taste

Szechuan Pepper Butter

2 cups bread crumbs

1 pound butter

4 tablespoons Szechuan brown peppercorns

4 tablespoons coarse cracked black peppercorns

½ cup shallots, minced

4 teaspoons garlic, minced

Salt and pepper to taste

SZECHUAN PEPPER BROILED SALMON
with Cilantro Crème Sauce
Serves 6 to 8

Mix white wine, sour cream, cilantro, green peppercorns and lime juice. Season with salt and pepper to taste, set aside.

Use a food processor to puree the bread crumbs, butter, peppercorns, shallots and garlic; salt and pepper to taste.

Brush salmon liberally with the Szechuan Butter. Broil over a hot mesquite (or similar) charcoal fire until slightly undercooked, about 8 to 10 minutes. Remove from the grill and place in a shallow pan. Top with more of the butter and brown under a broiler. Serve on top of the Cilantro Crème with lime slices as garnish.

Chanterelle and Leek Saute

Serves 4

In a large saute pan, heat the oil until it turns blue. Add garlic and shallots, stir constantly. When they become golden brown, add the marsala, lemon juice and chicken stock. Reduce the mixture by ½ on a steady simmer. Add the mushrooms and leeks; continue to reduce until the mushrooms and leeks are cooked through, 3 to 5 minutes. Remove from the pan and place on a warm serving dish.

Whisk the softened butter into the pan and season to taste with salt and pepper. Arrange the basil leaves on the mushrooms and leeks and top with the sauce; garnish with lemon and basil.

Chanterelle and Leek Saute
1 teaspoon olive oil
1 teaspoon garlic, minced
1 teaspoon shallots, minced
1 cup marsala wine
2 teaspoons lemon juice
1 cup chicken stock
1 pound chanterelle mushrooms,
  sliced
1 cup leeks, julienne
2 tablespoons butter, softened
Salt and pepper to taste
1 cup whole fresh basil leaves
Lemon slices and basil,
  for garnish

Spiced and Roasted Hazelnuts

Yield, about 4 cups

Preheat oven to 400°.

Spread nuts on a sheet pan and roast until golden, turning occasionally. Stir in seasoning ingredients to taste.

Spiced and Roasted Hazelnuts
2 pounds hazelnuts
Sugar, salt and pepper to taste
Honey
Tabasco or red chili paste
Pureed garlic

White Ganache Covered Reisling-Poached Pears

Serves 6

Combine Reisling, sugar and spices in a non-corroding saucepan and bring to a simmer.

Meanwhile, peel the pears as smoothly as possible, leaving the stems in place; remove the core through the bottom of the pear. Place the pears in the simmering syrup and poach until they are tender, about 20 minutes. Remove the pears from the syrup and set aside to cool.

Strain the poaching syrup and return it to the saucepan. Reduce to a medium syrup stage and remove from the heat. In a separate pan, bring the heavy cream to a low boil, remove from heat. Stir in the white chocolate gradually until all is dissolved and a smooth ganache is reached.

Pat the pears dry and cut a small portion off each base so they will stand upright. Place them in a shallow dish or pan and carefully ladle the ganache over each to achieve a smooth coating. Allow the pears to cool completely. Serve on dessert plates with the poaching syrup around each and a mint sprig for garnish.

White Ganache Covered
Reisling-Poached Pears
1 bottle of Reisling
2 cups sugar
4 whole cloves
2 bay leaves
1 vanilla bean, whole
6 whole ripe Bartlett pears
1 cup heavy cream
10 ounces white chocolate
6 mint sprigs, for garnish

The Heathman Hotel

The Homestead

HOT SPRINGS, VIRGINIA

While the Homestead's origins as a spa date to the George Washington and Thomas Jefferson eras of Virginia history, it was in 1891 that the modern Homestead was born. In that year a syndicate, under the direction of former Chesapeake and Ohio Railway Company President M. E. Ingalls, purchased the land on which the current Homestead—beautifully constructed of Kentucky red brick in the colonial style—is located. Crystal chandeliers and Corinthian columns lend stateliness to the famous Great Hall with its 24-foot ceilings and nearly the length of a football field at 240 feet. Ten American presidents have visited this vast, beautiful resort.

All recipes reprinted with permission from Dining at the Homestead, *copyright by Albert J. Schnarwyler, Eleanor E. Ferguson and James G. Ferguson, Jr., 1989.*

ROAST LOIN OF PORK STUFFED WITH APRICOTS
Serves 6 to 8

Native to Armenia, the apricot was discovered by the Romans while on campaign. The first mention of combining pork with apricots came from Apicius in De Re Coquinaria, *wherein apricots, dried dill, mint and cumin were simmered with the meat. Here, apricots fill the center of the roast and rosemary seasons the outside, providing a contrast of flavors as appealing as the look of the slices. Any leftover pork, sliced thinly, makes a delicious cold luncheon dish.*

Pork has been a favorite southern dish for generations, and this recipe has been a favorite of Homestead guests for decades.

Trim the loin of all but 1 inch of flank. Use a sharp knife to make a hole in the center of the loin all the way through, end to end. Enlarge the hole using a bulb baster (bulb removed) pushed through the opening, or use a boning knife with a twisting motion. Use your fingers to push as many of the dried apricots into the cavity as possible to make a compact stuffing. Tie the loin at 2-inch intervals with kitchen string.

Preheat oven to 350°.

Mix together salt, pepper and lemon rind, add rosemary. Rub the

Photo, plate 14

Roast Loin of Pork Stuffed with Apricots

1 boneless pork loin, about 3 pounds

4 ounces dried apricots

For seasoning blend:

½ teaspoon salt

½ teaspoon fresh ground black pepper

Grated rind of 1 lemon

½ teaspoon fresh rosemary, coarsely cut

For the vegetables:

½ medium onion, rough chopped

1 stalk celery, rough chopped

½ carrot, peeled, rough chopped

1 cup dry white wine

(continued, next page)

seasoning mixture all over the pork loin, working into the fat and meat.

Set the loin, fat side up, in a roasting pan; roast for 20 minutes. Reduce heat to 325° and roast an additional 20 minutes.

Drain the fat from the pan, strew the vegetables around the loin; roast for another 20 minutes. Pour the wine around the loin, continue roasting 25 minutes more (total roasting time—about 1 hour and 25 minutes; 25 to 30 minutes per pound). When done, cut away strings and set roast topside down on platter. Allow to rest in warm (not hot) area for 15 to 20 minutes.

For sauce, set roasting pan over medium heat. Use a wire whisk to blend cream, mustard and demi-glace into the drippings and vegetables. Simmer to reduce liquid by about ½, or until a light, creamy consistency is achieved (about 10 minutes); strain into a saucepan, adjust seasonings if necessary. Add any juices that may have escaped to the serving platter; keep warm.

Slice the loin for serving. Spoon sauce on warm plates, arrange slices neatly on the sauce, garnish with rosemary. Serve at once.

Dijon Cream Sauce
1 cup whipping cream
1 tablespoon Dijon mustard
½ cup demi-glace

BAKED OYSTERS WITH CRABMEAT GRATINÉE HOMESTEAD

Serves 2

Preheat oven to 325°.

In a small bowl, use a rubber spatula to gently blend crabmeat with ¼ cup of seafood sauce, caring not to break the lumps. Spread 1 tablespoon of the mixture over each oyster on the half shell, top with ½ teaspoon seafood sauce. Sprinkle with grated parmesan.

Nestle the oysters in a layer of rock salt in a baking dish. Bake for 6 minutes, then broil just long enough to get a golden glaze. Serve hot.

Oysters with Crabmeat
4 ounces lump crabmeat, cleaned
⅜ cup Homestead Seafood Sauce (page 123)
8 fresh oysters on the half shell
1½ tablespoons grated parmesan cheese
Rock salt for baking dish

ENGLISH BEEF TEA

a special broth—the perfect complement to an elegant menu

Serves 8 to 10

Divide the meat between 2½-gallon wide-mouth, heavy-duty glass jars, ladle broth over meat.

Fold about 12 pages of newspaper to fit the bottom of a large stockpot; insert the jars, add water to ⅔ the way up the side of the jars, set over low heat. When boil is achieved, set to low simmer. Cook for 5 hours (check occasionally to maintain water level).

Set a cheesecloth lined sieve over a mixing bowl and carefully pour the hot beef tea into it (do not disturb the solids—leave about 1 inch liquid in bottom of each jar).

To serve, reheat Tea gently until hot, but below simmering point. If needed, adjust seasoning with salt and Aromat. Remove any visible floating fat with a paper towel drawn across the surface. Ladle into warm serving dishes.

English Beef Tea
5 pounds extra-lean beef (shank or chuck), freshly ground
6 cups beef broth at room temperature
Dash salt
Dash Knorr Aromat

The Homestead

Ratatouille of Zucchini

Ratatouille of Zucchini

1½ pounds zucchini,
thinly sliced

½ medium green bell pepper,
thinly sliced

½ medium onion, thinly sliced

1 recipe Stewed Tomatoes
(page 123)

⅓ cup olive oil

Pinch fresh thyme, chopped

⅓ bay leaf

1 clove garlic, peeled and pressed

Salt and fresh ground black
pepper

½ cup grated parmesan cheese

Ratatouille of Zucchini
Serves 4 to 6

Preheat oven to 350°.

In mixing bowl, combine zucchini, green pepper, onion and stewed tomatoes; add olive oil, thyme, bay leaf and garlic. Salt and pepper to taste, blend thoroughly; pour into baking dish, sprinkle with parmesan cheese.

Cover loosely with aluminum foil, bake for 45 minutes; remove foil, bake 15 minutes more. Dip out any excess oil before serving.

Gateau Chambord

Gateau Chambord

1 recipe Génoise à la Vanille
(page 121)

Unsweetened framboise, for
brushing

2 cups raspberry puree
(page 122)

1 cup sugar

Juice of ½ lemon

2 cups whipping cream

2 teaspoons vanilla extract

1⅔ tablespoons unflavored
gelatin

½ cup unsweetened framboise

1 cup raspberry jelly, melted

2½ ounces sliced almonds,
lightly oven-browned

Gateau Chambord
Serves 16

Prepare Génoise, allow to cool completely.

Line bottom and sides of a 10-inch cake pan with waxed paper, letting paper stand 1 inch above pan edge (a dab of soft butter or peanut butter under the paper will hold it in place).

Use a serrated knife to evenly slice Génoise into 2 layers; brush each with framboise. Set 1 in cake pan, cut side up; tightly wrap the other layer, reserve in refrigerator.

In small mixing bowl, combine raspberry puree, sugar and lemon juice. Whisk until sugar is dissolved, reserve.

Beat cream and vanilla with electric mixer until stiff, refrigerate.

In small saucepan, whisk gelatin into framboise; when softened, heat until dissolved. Pour mixture into raspberry puree, whisk well. Use a rubber spatula to fold in the whipped cream, reserving ¾ cup. Pour the mixture onto the cake in the pan and chill until firm (about ½ hour). When firm, set the other cake layer on top, refrigerate for at least 3 hours.

Remove cake from pan, set on serving plate; brush top of cake with melted raspberry jelly. Mask the sides of the cake with reserved whipped cream, sprinkle top with roasted almonds.

The cake may be refrigerated for up to 2 hours before serving.

Photography: Bill Zeldis

COLOR PLATE 9
Garlic-Grilled Santa Barbara Spot Prawns, page 25
El Encanto Hotel and Garden Villas, Santa Barbara, California

COLOR PLATE 10
Roast Chicken Breast Greenbrier Valley, page 28
The Greenbrier, White Sulphur Springs, West Virginia

Photography: Barry Berenson

COLOR PLATE 11
Veal Hawthorne, page 31
Hawthorne Hotel, Salem, Massachusetts

Photography: Kanji Takeno

COLOR PLATE 12
Maryland Crab Cakes with Fennel Sauce, page 34
The Hay-Adams Hotel, Washington, D.C.

Photography: Bruce Forrester

COLOR PLATE 13
Grilled Medallions of Venison, page 37
The Heathman Hotel, Portland, Oregon

Photography: Romulo Yanes

COLOR PLATE 14
Roast Loin of Pork Stuffed with Apricots, page 40
The Homestead, Hot Springs, Virginia

Photography: George Johnson

COLOR PLATE 15
Venison with Stone Fruits and Berry Sauce, page 43
Hotel Atop The Bellevue, Philadelphia, Pennsylvania

Photography: Du Pont External Affairs

COLOR PLATE 16
Crabmeat Chesapeake Bay, page 46
Hotel du Pont, Wilmington, Delaware

Hotel Atop The Bellevue

PHILADELPHIA, PENNSYLVANIA

In 1902, George Boldt decided to build a hotel "of true opulence and splendor," in downtown Philadelphia, and thus began the $8 million construction of the Bellevue-Stratford, which opened September 20, 1904 across from the original Bellevue on Walnut Street. Designed in the French Renaissance style, the building contained ballrooms considered the most magnificent in the United States, lighting fixtures custom designed by Thomas Edison, and the most celebrated staircases in the city. Today the top seven floors of the National Historic Landmark have been exceptionally restored and rechristened "Hotel Atop The Bellevue."

VENISON SERVED WITH STONE FRUITS AND BERRY SAUCE
Serves 2

The Bellevue—one of the world's best known hotels for generations—maintained a reputation for fine hospitality and an ambience beyond the ordinary. Today, this revitalized hostelry continues that revered tradition with dining experiences that are truly exceptional; unique dishes with colors, textures and flavors guaranteed to entice even the most jaded palate.

For sauce: slightly reduce fruit juices and shallots in a large saucepan. Add stock, bay leaf and thyme. Reduce by ½ and strain, season with salt and pepper to taste.

Saute venison medallions quickly in 2 tablespoons butter (cook to medium rare). Remove medallions and deglaze the pan with sauce. Add fruit (raspberries last). Finish with butter and season with salt and pepper.

Photo, plate 15
Venison Served with Stone Fruits and Berry Sauce
Berry Sauce
2 cups cranberry juice
2 cups pineapple juice
1 teaspoon shallots
2 quarts venison stock, heated
1 bay leaf
1 sprig fresh thyme
Salt and pepper to taste
Venison
4 2-ounce venison medallions
2 tablespoons butter
2 peaches, cut in wedges
2 apricots, cut in wedges
¼ cup raspberries
½ pound butter

Grilled Calamari Salad

*1½ pounds squid, cleaned
  (page 123)*
*1¼ cups lemon juice (about 5
  lemons)*
1 small shallot
*1½ cups lemon-garlic oil (steep
  1 large head garlic and zest of
  1 lemon in ¾ cup olive oil and
  ¾ cup peanut oil 48 hours
  prior to serving)*
1 tablespoon green pepper, diced
1 tablespoon yellow pepper, diced
1 teaspoon capers
1 tablespoon cilantro, chopped
1 teaspoon lemon zest
Salt and pepper to taste
1½ pounds broccoli spears
*Lemon zest, whole cilantro
  leaves, whole roasted garlic
  cloves and julienne of tomato
  for garnish*

GRILLED CALAMARI SALAD
grilled squid with warm broccoli and roasted garlic
Serves 4

Grill squid over high heat until ¾ done. Squid cooks quickly ... it should require no more than 30 to 40 seconds on a hot grill, perhaps less. Squid is done when it turns milky white. For these purposes, it will lose its translucency, but not yet be opaque.

Reserve 4 whole small bodies for garnish and slice remainder. Marinate sliced squid for 20 minutes in ¾ cup lemon juice.

Whisk ½ cup lemon juice with chopped shallot and lemon-garlic oil to form dressing. Chill.

Drain squid and discard juice. Remarinate squid in new dressing with remaining ingredients. Steam broccoli for 2 minutes, plunge in ice water, then lightly saute in lemon-garlic oil.

Serve topped with the squid and warmed garnish.

Veal and Prawns

*12 1-ounce (jumbo) prawns
  (or shrimp)*
½ cup olive oil
Juice of 2 limes
*2 tablespoons tarragon,
  fresh chopped*
*12 2-ounce veal tenderloin
  medallions*
2 tablespoons olive oil
2 large shallots, finely chopped
½ cup madeira
1 cup veal stock
¼ cup heavy cream
3 sprigs fresh tarragon, finely cut
Lemon juice, for basting
*Fresh tarragon sprigs, for
  garnish*

VEAL AND PRAWNS — FLEUR D'ESTRAGON
Serves 6

Remove prawns' shells, leaving bodies and ends of tails; marinate 2 hours or longer in mixture of olive oil, lime juice and tarragon, turning frequently.

Saute veal medallions in 2 tablespoons olive oil for 2 minutes each, turning once; set aside. In same pan, saute the shallots lightly. Add madeira, flame to remove alcohol. Deglaze pan with veal stock. Stir in the cream and add the fresh cut tarragon. Replace the medallions and cook for 1 to 2 minutes over low heat.

Meanwhile, grill the prawns rapidly on both sides, basting lightly with lemon juice.

Glaze each serving plate with the sauce. Place 2 medallions in the center with the prawns on each side. Garnish with tarragon.

Roasted Red Pepper Soup

with boursin cheese

Serves 6

Preheat oven to 400°.

Coat bell pepper, onion and garlic with olive oil, roast until pepper is wrinkled and loses its gloss (about 15 minutes). Deseed, peel and chop the bell pepper; peel and chop garlic; chop onion. Saute them gently in the butter.

Add chicken stock, then the cream. Add the thyme and simmer for 10 minutes.

Season with salt and pepper and serve with crumbled boursin cheese.

Robert's Apple Pie

Yield, 1 10-inch deep-dish pie

Mix together flour, nuts and salt. Cut in shortening to make a crumbly mixture. Add ice water a little at a time, blending into a smooth dough; chill. Split dough in half. Roll out to fit a 10-inch deep-dish pan and the other half to cover.

Preheat oven to 375°.

Mix together sugar, flour, cinnamon, nutmeg and cornstarch. Toss apples in dry mix. Layer apple slices in pie crust using all (it will be stacked high), place butter on top. Egg-wash edges of bottom crust, place on top. Seal edges. Bake for approximately 30 minutes.

Remove from oven. Cut 1-inch hole in center of top while still bubbly hot. Pour in Crème Anglaise. Put back in oven and bake until golden brown or apples are done, approximately 20 additional minutes.

Roasted Red Pepper Soup

3 red bell peppers
½ Bermuda onion
6 large cloves garlic, unpeeled
Olive oil, for coating
2 tablespoons butter
5 cups chicken stock
2 cups heavy cream
1 large sprig fresh thyme
Salt and pepper
2 ounces boursin cheese, crumbled

Robert's Apple Pie
Walnut Pie Crust

2 cups all-purpose flour
1 cup walnuts, finely chopped
1 teaspoon salt
1 cup vegetable shortening
⅓ cup ice water
Apple filling:
2 cups sugar
¼ cup flour
1½ tablespoons cinnamon
⅛ teaspoon nutmeg
1½ tablespoons cornstarch
10 to 12 Granny Smith apples, peeled, cored, cut in ⅛-inch slices
3 tablespoons butter
1 egg mixed with 1 tablespoon water, for egg wash
½ cup Crème Anglaise (page 120)

Hotel Atop The Bellevue

Hotel du Pont

WILMINGTON, DELAWARE

Since opening in 1913, the Hotel du Pont has been a Wilmington landmark. Conceived to provide the city with a hotel of prestige, the public spaces alone required the labors of 18 French and Italian craftsmen for almost two and one-half years, who carved, painted, gilded and laid the intricate marble and mosaic floors. A master achievement, the Hotel du Pont was rightfully proclaimed a rival to the finest in Europe. The exceptional interiors have been further enhanced by the hotel's support of the arts, decorated with more than 800 original paintings representing the talents of some 250 artists, including three generations of Wyeths.

❧

CRABMEAT CHESAPEAKE BAY
with Tomato Basil Coulis

The Atlantic blue crab or Callinectus *is Greek for "beautiful swimmer." Though the beauty of their appearance remains debatable, no one can dispute their enormous popularity. No body of water has been more intensely fished for crabs than the Chesapeake Bay. Traditionally, the crabbing centers of Maryland's Eastern Shore picked the crabmeat by hand. Today, more and more machines are used in the processing. Since the mid-19th century, the Bay's blue crab fishery has made the United States one of the leading crab consuming nations of the world.*

Core tomatoes and cross-cut top; place in boiling water for 30 seconds. Remove, place in cold water to loosen skins, peel. Halve tomatoes, squeeze out seeds, then dice. Heat pan; add olive oil and diced tomatoes. Simmer shortly, add basil, salt and pepper to taste, simmer 2 minutes. Place coulis on plate.

Melt butter in small pan, gently saute crabmeat so lumps don't fall apart; sprinkle with white wine, remove from heat. Place crabmeat in center of coulis, garnish with fresh basil leaves and serve.

You may also serve boiled potatoes on the side.

Photo, plate 16
Crabmeat Chesapeake Bay
For each serving:
Tomato Basil Coulis
2 medium tomatoes
2 tablespoons extra virgin olive oil
3 leaves fresh basil, julienne; reserving top leaves for garnish
Salt and pepper
Crabmeat Chesapeake
1 tablespoon sweet butter
4 ounces lump crabmeat
Dry white wine
Basil leaves, for garnish

CREAM OF PUMPKIN SOUP WITH CURRY

Serves 12

Melt butter in 6- or 8-quart saucepan over medium-high heat.

Add onion and saute for 5 minutes until translucent. Add curry powder and cook for 2 more minutes. Add chicken stock, pumpkin, brown sugar, salt, pepper and nutmeg; blend in cream. Cook over medium heat for 10 minutes.

Adjust to desired consistency with roux (equal parts melted butter and flour) or a whitewash (flour and water). If too thin, cook an additional 10 minutes to cook out the starch. If too thick, add more cream. Adjust flavor with seasonings.

Blend in a blender until smooth and creamy. Ladle into bowls and garnish with chives or parsley.

Cream of Pumpkin Soup
4 tablespoons butter
½ cup onion, chopped
1 tablespoon curry powder
1½ quarts chicken stock
32 ounces (4 cups) canned pumpkin
⅔ cup brown sugar
Salt to taste
White pepper to taste
Nutmeg to taste
2 cups heavy cream
Chives or parsley, chopped, for garnish

CINNAMON PARFAIT WITH FIGS AND CASSIS

Serves 12

Combine sugar, egg yolks and vanilla in mixing bowl, whip at high speed until thick and frothy; fold in whipped cream, add Frangelico. Add cinnamon a little at a time until desired flavor is achieved.

Pour into coffee cups or timbale-shaped molds and freeze.

Put figs in saucepan. Add sugar, wine and cassis. Cook slowly until figs are cooked soft, remove from liquid. Reduce liquid to a syrup consistency.

To unmold parfait, dip cups or molds in hot water, invert onto serving plate. Garnish with 1 warm fig and a few tablespoons of the warm syrup.

Cinnamon Parfait
2 cups sugar
18 egg yolks
1½ teaspoons vanilla extract
1½ quarts heavy cream, whipped
Frangelico liqueur
2 to 3 tablespoons ground cinnamon, to taste
12 fresh figs
2 cups sugar
2 cups red wine
2 cups cassis

Historic Perspective

Thomas Jefferson's interest in foods was well known: he designed expansive gardens at Monticello and wrote one of America's most popular early cookbooks. While in the White House, he was known to make a daily trip to Georgetown to select his own fruits and vegetables. His White House maitre d'hotel, Etienne Lemaire, is credited with introducing to America the fine French art of cooking with wine.

Each morning Jefferson conferred with Lemaire regarding the menu for the 14 or more guests expected that evening for supper. Benjamin Latrobe, the Baltimorean who designed the Capitol, was a frequent guest. He noted:

"There is a degree of ease in Mr. Jefferson's company that everyone seems to feel and enjoy." There were three table rules: "No healths" (because the courteous return of a toast could continue until everyone was quite drunk), "no politics, and no restraint."

Hotel Hershey

HERSHEY, PENNSYLVANIA

The Hotel Hershey is the legacy of chocolate king Milton Hershey, whose "Great Building Campaign" was designed to employ the town's construction workers during the Depression. Completed in 1933, the hotel was described by late world traveler Lowell Thomas as a "palace that out-palaces the palaces of the Maharajahs of India." Styled after the famous 19th-century grand hotels of the Mediterranean, its noted architecture features a Spanish-influenced galleried lobby with a hand-sculpted fountain, tiled floors and a wide, oak-railed mezzanine. Some public rooms include stained-glass windows, many offering vistas of the 20 acres of manicured formal gardens, reflecting pools and fountains.

SUPREME CHOCOLATE ALMOND TORTE
Yield, 1 10-inch cake

The pastry shop at The Hotel Hershey has produced and created the decorative Supreme Chocolate Almond Torte for a very special occasion. This dark, rich, elegant dessert is the perfect ending to a perfect evening.

The recipe for the cake originated in the Hershey Foods Test Kitchen utilizing a new Dutch-processed cocoa called Hershey's European Style Cocoa. The Hotel Hershey became interested in the product as a great addition to the fine foods produced with a Continental flair. The Hotel Hershey had the opportunity to share this recipe with a national gathering of Food Writers and Consultants which was hosted by Hershey Chocolate, U.S.A. The acclaim was instant, and everyone thoroughly enjoyed this regal, dense chocolate dessert.

Heat oven to 350°.

In a large mixing bowl, beat together butter and sugar until creamy. Add eggs, 1 at a time, until well blended. Add vanilla and salt.

Sift together cocoa and flour. Beat into butter mixture. Stir in almonds.

Pour into a 10-inch cake pan. Bake 45 minutes or until a wooden pick inserted in center comes out clean. Remove cake from pan; cool thoroughly.

Frost with Chocolate Buttercream. Glaze with Sacher Glaze.

Photo, plate 17
Chocolate Almond Torte
1¼ cups butter
1¾ cups sugar
4 eggs
1½ teaspoons vanilla extract
Dash salt
2¼ ounces HERSHEY'S Premium European Style Cocoa
½ cup plus 1 tablespoon all-purpose flour
4 ounces ground toasted almonds
Chocolate Buttercream (page 50)
Sacher Glaze (page 50)

Chocolate Buttercream

Chocolate Buttercream

1 pound 4 ounces (2½ cups)
  unsalted butter
4 cups confectioners' sugar
1½ cups vegetable shortening
1 cup cream fondant
1½ teaspoons vanilla extract
8 ounces HERSHEY'S semi-sweet
  chocolate chips, melted
2 to 3 ounces warm water

CHOCOLATE BUTTERCREAM

Yield, 3 pounds

In a large mixer bowl, beat butter and sugar well. Add shortening, fondant and vanilla extract. Beat until creamy and very smooth. Add chocolate and water, if desired, to adjust consistency.

Sacher Glaze

8 ounces HERSHEY'S semi-sweet
  chocolate chips
½ cup unsalted butter

SACHER GLAZE

Yield, 1½ cups

Melt together chips and butter. Blend until smooth.

White Chocolate Mousse Torte

1 pound white chocolate
  couveture, chopped
⅓ cup water
¼ cup brandy
2½ packets gelatin
6 eggs, separated
⅔ cup sugar, divided
6 10-inch round yellow cake
  (Gènoise) layers (page 121)
21 ounces (2½ cups plus
  2 tablespoons) heavy cream,
  beaten to soft peaks
White chocolate shavings
Raspberry Sauce (page 122)

WHITE CHOCOLATE MOUSSE TORTE

with Raspberry Sauce

Yield, 3 10-inch cakes or 48 servings

In bowl over warm water, melt white chocolate.

In saucepan, combine water and brandy. Over low heat, dissolve gelatin in water mixture until mixture is clear. Add gelatin mixture to white chocolate (chocolate will become stiff, but continue stirring until smooth).

In mixer bowl, beat egg yolks and ⅓ cup sugar until fluffy.

In separate clean bowl, beat egg whites until foamy. Gradually add remaining ⅓ cup sugar, beating until soft peaks form.

Fold chocolate mixture into beaten egg yolks. Fold egg yolk mixture into beaten egg whites. Fold egg white mixture into whipped cream.

Place 1 cake layer in each of 3 10-inch cake pans or rings. Fill each pan with mousse filling, dividing evenly. Top with second cake layer.

Refrigerate until firm, or freeze.

Just before serving, frost cake with whipped cream. Cover with white chocolate shavings. Serve with Raspberry Sauce.

CHOCOLATE CHEESECAKE
Yield, 3 10-inch cakes

Heat oven to 300°.

In large mixer bowl, beat together cream cheese and sugar until smooth. Add eggs, 1 at a time, blending well after each addition. Blend until smooth. Add melted chocolate. Blend well. Add Kahlua. Gradually add heavy cream, blending well.

Cover bottom of 3 10-inch springform cake pans with chocolate cookie crumbs or graham cracker crumbs. Fill each pan with batter, dividing evenly. Bake in water bath for 1 hour.

CHOCOLATE MOUSSE
Serves 12

In bowl over warm water, melt chocolate. Stir warm water and Kirschwasser into melted chocolate.

In mixer bowl, beat egg yolks and ¼ cup sugar until thickened. Fold into chocolate mixture.

In separate bowl, beat egg whites until foamy. Gradually beat in remaining ¼ cup sugar until soft peaks form. Fold into chocolate and egg yolk mixture.

In mixer bowl, beat heavy cream until soft peaks form. Fold into chocolate mixture.

Fill champagne or wine glasses with chocolate mousse. Garnish with chocolate shavings.

CHOCOLATE SABAYON CAKE
Yield, 1 10-inch cake

In a large bowl over warm water, whip egg yolks and sugar until thick and lemon-colored.

In a small bowl, combine gelatin and water. Let stand until gelatin is dissolved.

In top of double boiler over hot boiling water, melt chocolate chips. Stir in sherry and gelatin mixture until smooth. Stir in egg yolk mixture.

In large mixer bowl, beat heavy cream and sugar until soft peaks form. Add vanilla to taste. Fold into chocolate mixture.

Place 1 cake layer in bottom of 10-inch cake pan or ring. Fill with chocolate sabayon. Top with second cake layer. Refrigerate until firm, or freeze. Just before serving, frost cake with Chocolate Buttercream and coat with chocolate shavings.

Chocolate Cheesecake

3¾ pounds cream cheese
2⅔ cups sugar
8 eggs
1 pound 4 ounces HERSHEY'S
  semi-sweet chocolate chips,
  melted
¼ cup Kahlua
1 quart plus 3½ cups
  heavy cream
Chocolate cookie crumbs or
  graham cracker crumbs

Chocolate Mousse

8 ounces HERSHEY'S semi-sweet
  chocolate, chopped
1½ ounces HERSHEY'S
  unsweetened baking chocolate,
  chopped
¼ cup warm water
2 tablespoons Kirschwasser
5 eggs, separated
½ cup granulated sugar, divided
1 pint heavy cream
Chocolate shavings, for garnish

Chocolate Sabayon Cake

¾ cup egg yolks
½ cup sugar
⅔ ounce (3 packets) gelatin
⅔ cup water
8 ounces HERSHEY'S
  semi-sweet chocolate chips
¾ cup plus 2 tablespoons sherry
3 cups heavy cream
Confectioners' sugar
Vanilla extract to taste
2 10-inch chocolate cake layers
  (page 120)
Chocolate Buttercream
  (page 50)
Chocolate shavings

Hotel Hershey

Hotel Northampton

NORTHAMPTON, MASSACHUSETTS

The rich heritage of the Hotel Northampton, built in 1927, owes much to its first manager, Lewis Wiggins. An avid collector of American antiques, Wiggins sought to achieve museum status for the hotel's public rooms and furnishings. By 1937 he employed a full-time antiquarian-curator with a staff of 15. Created from an adjacent century-old structure, the authentic, colonial-styled Wiggins Tavern opened in 1930; in its courtyard the Old Country Store was built, furnished and stocked as a store would have been before 1850. Today's fully-refurbished guest rooms feature feather duvets and wicker accents, with classic furnishings in Chippendale, Federal and Duncan Phyfe styles.

Photo, plate 18

Indian Pudding

¾ cup yellow cornmeal

¼ cup black molasses

¼ cup New England maple
  syrup

¼ cup butter, softened

¼ teaspoon salt

¼ teaspoon baking soda

2 eggs, beaten

½ teaspoon cinnamon
  (optional)

¼ teaspoon nutmeg (optional)

¼ cup sugar

6 cups hot milk

Vanilla ice cream or whipped
  cream for topping

INDIAN PUDDING
Serves 8 to 10

Indian pudding is the oldest New England dessert on record. Cornmeal was originally called Indian meal, a gift to the colonists from the Indians. The early version of this recipe probably came about when all cooking centered around a fireplace or a woodburning stove, and the pudding was allowed to slowly bake over the smouldering embers.

As long as we can historically recollect, Indian pudding has been on our Wiggins Tavern menu and remains a continued "ole' time favorite." There are many variations of this recipe, but ours has been handed down from chef to chef and we think our combination of dark molasses and true New England maple syrup creates a delicate sweetness known only to us!

Preheat oven to 400°.

Mix the cornmeal with all ingredients, add 3 cups hot milk, stirring carefully. Place mixture in a 2½- to 3-quart bean pot or other covered casserole, bake until the mixture comes to a boil.

Reduce oven to 275°. Stir the remaining hot milk into the pudding, bake covered for an additional 4 to 6 hours until all milk is absorbed. Stir every half hour.

Serve hot with ice cream or whipped cream.

BAKED SNOW CRAB STUFFED SHRIMP
Serves 4

In saute pan, melt butter, add crab, cream, sherry, salt and pepper; simmer 5 minutes. Add roux and simmer additional 5 minutes, remove from heat. Add bread crumbs, mix thoroughly. Spread mixture on a cookie sheet, cool in refrigerator.

Preheat oven to 350°.

Stuff each shrimp with about 4½ tablespoons of the stuffing, folding tails upward and to the front. Divide shrimp into 4 small casserole dishes. Combine lemon juice and wine, sprinkle over the shrimp (add any remaining liquid to the bottom of the casserole dishes), top with buttered bread crumbs. Bake for 10 to 15 minutes, being cautious not to overbake. Shrimp should be pink, but not dry.

Serve with clarified butter and a favorite vegetable and potato.

Snow Crab Stuffed Shrimp
1 cup butter
1 pound snow crab, thawed
1 cup heavy cream
4 tablespoons sherry
Salt and pepper to taste
2 teaspoons roux (a paste of
 equal parts flour and butter)
3 cups bread crumbs
20 jumbo shrimp (15 count),
 peeled and deveined, tail
 remaining
¼ cup lemon juice
¾ cup white wine
For buttered crumbs, mix:
1 cup bread crumbs
¼ cup melted butter
½ teaspoon paprika
Salt and pepper to taste

YANKEE POT ROAST
Serves 8 to 10

Preheat oven to 275°.

Spread all of the onion, celery and carrots on the bottom of a large Dutch oven. Rub roast with garlic and sprinkle with salt and pepper. Place roast on top of vegetables in center of pan and add water until pan is ¾ filled, roast, uncovered, for 2 hours. Turn roast and cook another 2 hours, or until the internal temperature is 170°.

Take roast out of pan and place on serving dish. Drain all stock and juices through a colander into a saucepan. You should have enough stock to equal 2 to 3 cups. If necessary, add beef broth. Bring liquid to a simmer. Meanwhile, melt the butter in a small saucepan. Add the flour and stir to form a roux; slowly stir into stock to thicken for gravy.

Yankee Pot Roast
1 pound yellow onions, diced
½ pound celery, diced
½ pound carrots, diced
1 4- to 5-pound eye round roast
1 tablespoon garlic, minced
1 teaspoon salt
1 teaspoon black pepper, crushed
2 tablespoons butter
2 tablespoons flour or cornstarch

Hotel Northampton

Chicken Pot Pie

12 ounces chicken breast, cooked,
cut into ½-inch chunks
½ cup celery, diced
½ cup carrots, par-cooked, diced
½ cup yellow onion, diced
1 cup red bliss potatoes,
parboiled, diced
2 cups chicken gravy, heated
2 eggs, beaten (egg wash)
2 7-inch pie crusts

CHICKEN POT PIE
Serves 2

Preheat oven to 375°.

In each of 2 6¾-inch round by 2¼-inch deep casserole dishes, layer all items, starting with chicken and ending with potatoes. Heat gravy and pour over top of chicken and vegetable mixture. Rub edges of casserole dishes with egg wash. Place pie crusts on top of casseroles and seal edges. Egg wash top crusts.

Bake for 25 to 30 minutes, or until crusts are lightly browned.

Original Recipe Pecan Pie

4 eggs
1¼ cups whole pecans
2 cups corn syrup
¼ cup molasses
¼ cup butter, melted
1 teaspoon vanilla extract
1 teaspoon salt
1 9- to 10-inch unbaked pie shell

ORIGINAL RECIPE PECAN PIE
Yield, 1 9- to 10-inch pie

Preheat oven to 450°.

Beat eggs well, add remaining ingredients, stirring until blended. Pour mixture into pie shell. Bake for approximately 40 minutes, until firm.

The Jefferson Sheraton

A blend of Beaux Arts and Renaissance Revival styles inspired by the Villa Medici, the Jefferson opened on Halloween, 1895, and was promptly hailed as one of the finest hotels in the country. Damaged by fire in 1901, the Jefferson reopened in 1907, enlarged and offering novel features including fish and alligator ponds in the Palm Court. Restored in 1986, The Jefferson Sheraton is a showcase of architectural detail: upper and lower lobbies with faux marble columns, stained glass skylights and the noted Edward V. Valentine sculpture of Thomas Jefferson. Particularly famous is the hotel's 36-step grand staircase, which some say inspired the great staircase in the movie *Gone With The Wind.*

ROAST PHEASANT STUFFED WITH OYSTERS AND VIRGINIA HAM
Serves 6

Many wild-fowl recipes utilized the Southern Ruffled Grouse until the introduction of the Chinese Ring-Necked Pheasant and the English Pheasant into the United States in the late 19th century, which hybridized and proliferated extensively. In England, the pheasant is raised in large numbers on game farms and released for hunting. Here, market-bound birds are also raised on farms, though a lively sport has developed around hunting those in the wild.

This delightful dish, both eye-appealing and rich in flavor, combines three of Virginia's "home grown" specialties: pheasant, Chesapeake oysters and world-famous Virginia ham.

Debone pheasants, reserving breasts and carcasses (legs may be cooked in the stock or used for other purposes).

Cook pheasant carcasses in chicken stock over medium heat until liquid reduces to 1 pint, strain. Check consistency; if necessary, thicken with mixture of cornstarch and water. In separate pot, cook shallots in port wine until reduced by ½, add pheasant stock, season to taste.

Photo, plate 19
Pheasant and Sauce
3 whole pheasants
4¾ quarts chicken stock
1 tablespoon cornstarch
1 tablespoon water
1 shallot, finely diced
1¼ cups port wine
Salt and pepper
2 tablespoons clarified butter
 or cooking oil, for frying
(Continued, page 56)

Oyster and Ham Stuffing

¼ cup butter
24 oysters, shucked
3 ounces Virginia ham, julienne
  (Smithfield may be substituted)
¼ cup onion, finely diced
2 tablespoons celery, finely diced
1 cup chicken stock
1 cup bread, diced
Salt and pepper

Virginia Peanut Soup

½ cup clarified butter
½ cup onion, finely diced
¼ cup celery, finely diced
¼ cup carrots, finely diced
6 cups shelled peanuts
1 quart chicken stock
¼ cup all-purpose flour
Salt and pepper

Raspberry Vinaigrette

Yield, 4½ cups
1 pint raspberries, fresh if
  available, pureed
¾ cup raspberry or red wine
  vinegar
1½ teaspoons basil, chopped
½ teaspoon oregano, chopped
½ teaspoon thyme, chopped
½ teaspoon shallot, finely diced
¼ teaspoon garlic, finely
  chopped
2 cups olive or high-grade
  vegetable oil
2 tablespoons sugar
Salt and pepper
(Continued, page 57)

Heat butter in large saute pan, add oysters and ham. When oysters are halfway cooked, stir in onion and celery. Add chicken stock and bread, season with salt and pepper, cool.

Make an incision in thickest part of each pheasant breast into the center, fill with Stuffing. Season breasts with salt and pepper.

Preheat oven to 375°.

Heat butter or oil in medium saute pan. Sear breasts on both sides until light brown. Remove to baking dish, bake 8 to 10 minutes until done.

Remove from oven; slice each breast 2 to 3 times on an angle, layer on serving plate. Ladle sauce over the breast, serve.

VIRGINIA PEANUT SOUP
Serves 6

Peanuts are the edible seeds of a tropical bean plant native to Brazil, now grown as far north as Virginia. Peanuts have been grown in the Southern states, in ever-increasing quantities, since the Civil War. Those grown in south-central Virginia are one of the state's most important agricultural products. Pigs raised in the town of Smithfield are fed a diet of peanuts, providing the distinctive flavor of the famed "Smithfield Hams".

Heat large stock pot. Add ¼ cup butter, onions, celery, carrots and ¼ of the peanuts. Saute, but do not brown; add chicken stock. In food processor, puree balance of peanuts into a paste, reserve.

Thicken stock with a roux made with the flour and remaining butter; bring to a boil, add pureed peanuts. Reduce heat and simmer for 1 hour.

At serving time, strain the soup, season to taste with salt and pepper.

BIBB AND ENDIVE SALAD WITH RASPBERRY VINAIGRETTE
Serves 6

Lettuce grows both wild and domesticated throughout the northern hemisphere. This fresh vinaigrette gives new life to this staple of the American dinner menu.

For the Raspberry Vinaigrette: whisk together raspberries, vinegar, herbs, shallots and garlic in medium mixing bowl, slowly adding oil. Adjust flavor with sugar to desired tartness; season with salt and pepper to taste.

For the Salad: cut end off endive, reserve leaves. Core the bibb lettuce, remove outer leaves; tear lettuce by hand into bite-sized pieces, rinse and drain thoroughly.

Arrange endive with points outward around border of serving plates. Place bibb in the middle, drizzle with Raspberry Vinaigrette, serve.

Bibb and Endive Salad
1 head Belgian endive
2 heads bibb (or butter) lettuce
Raspberry Vinaigrette (page 56)

VIRGINIA SPOON BREAD
Serves 6 to 8

Preheat oven to 350°.

Scald milk in saucepan (do not boil); remove from heat. Add cornmeal, whisking constantly until lump free, add butter; cool. When sufficiently cool, add egg yolks.

In separate bowl, whip egg whites until stiff peaks form, incorporating sugar halfway through the process. Fold egg whites into cornmeal mixture, season lightly with salt and pepper.

Place in small, greased, glass baking dish and bake until stiffened, 40 to 45 minutes. (Spoon bread is meant to be soft and fluffy, not as firm as corn bread.) Serve immediately.

Virginia Spoon Bread
2 cups whole milk
¾ cup cornmeal
1½ tablespoons butter
2 eggs, separated
2 teaspoons sugar
Salt and pepper to taste

PEAR TART
Serves 6

Preheat oven to 375°.

Heat sugar and water in medium saucepan. Core pears and cut in half lengthwise; simmer in sugar/water mixture until tender, remove and cool.

For custard, heat cream to boiling in small saucepan, remove from heat.

Place egg yolks, sugar and vanilla in mixing bowl (on top of double boiler), incorporate cream slowly so as not to scramble the eggs. Place mixture over boiling water and cook until thickened, stirring constantly (use a spoon, not a whisk). Remove from heat, chill quickly over ice, then refrigerate.

For Chocolate Sauce, heat cream to boiling in a small saucepan. Chip chocolate into small pieces, place in mixing bowl. Pour boiling cream over the chocolate, stir until melted. Keep warm, but not over direct heat.

Cut puff pastry into pear shapes, approximately twice the size of the pears; place on greased cookie sheet. Ladle 1 tablespoon of custard in center of each pastry base. Slice each pear widthwise and fan out over custard, allowing enough exposed pastry to puff around filling. Brush pastry with beaten egg mixture. Bake 8 to 10 minutes, until golden brown.

Place on plates, ladle Chocolate Sauce around the bottom of each tart. Garnish with mint leaves.

Pear Tart
1 cup sugar
2 cups water
3 pears
For custard:
1 cup heavy cream
6 egg yolks
1 tablespoon sugar
⅛ teaspoon vanilla extract
Chocolate Sauce
½ cup heavy cream
8 ounces semi-sweet chocolate

1 sheet puff pastry (from your grocer's freezer)
2 eggs, beaten
Fresh mint leaves for garnish (optional)

The Jefferson Sheraton

John Rutledge House Inn

CHARLESTON, SOUTH CAROLINA

A National Historic Landmark, the John Rutledge House was built in 1763 by John Rutledge, a noted signer of the U.S. Constitution. The inn incorporates two carriage houses plus the distinctive home. Restoration has enhanced the graceful ironwork and original elaborate interiors, which include carved Italian marble fireplaces and inlaid floors. Much of the history of South Carolina and the United States can be traced to meetings and writings which took place in the home's large second-floor ballroom and adjoining library. Reminders of Rutledge's service to state and nation can be found in the inn—particularly South Carolina's palmetto tree symbol and the Federal eagle in the antebellum ironwork.

RUTLEDGE HOUSE INN'S SHE-CRAB SOUP
Serves 4

She-Crab Soup, a Charleston delicacy, was created at the John Rutledge House. During a formal dinner in the 1920s given by Mayor and Mrs. R.G. Rhett, the butler was asked to dress up the pale soup generally served. He added the orange-hued crab eggs which improved the color and flavor. Thus began a tradition synonymous with Charleston cuisine.

Heat butter in large saucepan. Add celery, mace and pepper, saute until celery is translucent. Meanwhile, heat milk and chicken stock in small pan until hot, not boiling. Add flour to celery mixture, stirring to make a roux; let bubble gently for a few minutes, but do not brown. Slowly add milk/chicken stock mixture, salt to taste.

Add crabmeat, heavy cream, Worcestershire and sherry. Simmer for 30 minutes or until thickened to desired consistency.

(Optional) garnish each serving with egg and paprika.

Note on ingredients: "she-crabs" are regarded as a delicacy due to a flavor richer than "he-crabs", and "she's" orange-hued eggs give the soup additional flavor and color. She-crabs are difficult to find in many parts of the country, so white crabmeat may be substituted. Chopped hard-boiled egg yolk may be crumbled in the soup to imitate crab eggs.

Photo, plate 20

She-Crab Soup

5 tablespoons butter

½ cup celery, finely chopped

⅔ teaspoon mace

¼ teaspoon white pepper

3½ cups milk

½ cup chicken stock

5 tablespoons flour

2 cups crabmeat, cleaned

1 cup heavy cream

¼ cup Worcestershire

3 tablespoons sherry

Salt to taste

Optional garnish:

2 hard-boiled egg yolks, grated

Paprika

Kings Courtyard Inn

CHARLESTON, SOUTH CAROLINA

In the late 1600s and early 1700s, King Street was the main "trail" leading to old Charles Towne. Ever since, this quaint thoroughfare of shops and charming homes has delighted Charlestonians and visitors alike. Built in 1853, the 34-room Kings Courtyard Inn is one of Charleston's most historic inns. The three-story antebellum structure was designed by architect Francis D. Lee in the Greek Revival style, with unusual Egyptian detail. One of historic King Street's largest and oldest structures, the building has had many uses in its 140-year existence—high quality shops, private residences and, at one time, the upper floors were used as an inn catering to plantation owners, shipping interests and merchant guests.

SOUTH CAROLINA SEAFOOD CASSEROLE
Serves 6 to 8

Incredibly simple yet elegant enough for guests, this Atlantic coast favorite allows the rich flavors of its ingredients to come through.

Preheat oven to 350°.
Over medium heat, saute shrimp and scallops in butter until heated through, but not fully cooked, about 2 minutes. Blend all ingredients, pour into 8 x 11-inch pan, bake until edges are bubbly, about 30 minutes.

South Carolina
Seafood Casserole
1 pound shrimp, peeled,
* deveined, tails removed*
1 pound scallops
3 tablespoons butter
1 pound crabmeat, cleaned
2 cups cooked rice
1½ cups V8 juice
1½ cups mayonnaise
⅓ cup green bell pepper,
* chopped*
Salt and pepper to taste

Pumpkin Apple Muffins

2½ cups all-purpose flour

2 cups sugar

1 teaspoon baking soda

½ teaspoon salt

2 eggs, lightly beaten

1 cup canned pumpkin pie mix

½ cup vegetable oil

2 cups apples, peeled and
   finely chopped

Streusel topping:

1 cup pecans

1 cup golden raisins

2 tablespoons all-purpose flour

¼ cup brown sugar

½ teaspoon ground cinnamon

4 teaspoons butter

PUMPKIN APPLE STREUSEL MUFFINS
Yield, 18 to 24 muffins

pumpkins and apples—two American standbys—are featured ingredients of these tasty, easy-to-make muffins

Preheat oven to 350˚.

In a large bowl, combine first 4 ingredients, set aside. In medium bowl, combine eggs, pumpkin and oil. Add liquid ingredients to dry ingredients, stir until moistened. Stir in apples, spoon batter into greased or paper-lined muffin tins, filling ¾ full.

Blend together streusel ingredients; sprinkle topping over batter. Bake for 35 to 40 minutes, until golden brown.

Pumpkin Bread

3 cups sugar

1 cup vegetable oil

2 cups prepared pumpkin

3 eggs

3 cups all-purpose flour

1 teaspoon nutmeg

1 teaspoon ground cloves

1 teaspoon cinnamon

1 teaspoon baking powder

1 teaspoon baking soda

½ teaspoon salt

Optional additions:

½ cup raisins

½ cup chopped nuts

PUMPKIN BREAD
Yield, 2 9-inch loaves

Preheat oven to 350˚.

Mix sugar and oil, add pumpkin and eggs. In a larger bowl, mix flour with all remaining ingredients, add pumpkin/egg mixture, combine well.

Grease bottoms only of 9 x 5 x 3-inch loaf pans. Pour in batter, bake for 1 hour and 15 minutes, or until a toothpick inserted in center comes out clean. Cool 5 minutes, loosen sides of loaf; remove from pan.

Baked Artichoke Dip

1 8-ounce can artichoke hearts,
   drained

1 cup sour cream

1 cup mayonnaise

1 cup grated parmesan cheese

BAKED ARTICHOKE DIP
Yield, 4 cups

an easy to prepare, tasty spread for crackers and breads

Preheat oven to 325˚.

Chop artichokes, mix all ingredients. Bake 30 minutes, until bubbly.

La Concha—A Holiday Inn Hotel

KEY WEST, FLORIDA

A popular stopover for wealthy adventurers who enjoyed sportfishing, the nightlife and proximity to the casinos of Havana, Key West was reveling in the Roaring Twenties when the La Concha Hotel opened in January, 1926. Key West resident Ernest Hemingway was a regular guest; Tennessee Williams finished writing *A Streetcar Named Desire* while staying there. But the stock market crash, a hurricane and years of neglect led to the hotel's decline and closure. Restored in 1986, its award-winning rooms are nostalgically decorated with antiques, poster beds, wicker, and lace curtains. Again the "Grande Dame of Key West," the landmark hotel is listed in the National Register of Historic Places.

KEY LIME PIE
Serves 6 to 8

From the days when pirates and "wreckers" were the first inhabitants of Key West, the people who settled this small subtropical island have proven their resourcefulness in many ways. Native Keysters, or "Conchs", as they prefer to be called, have been a hardy and self-sufficient lot, able to withstand hurricanes, droughts and other adversities. Who else except a Key West "Conch" could transform the tart Key lime into a tropical treat requested by kings, presidents and visitors from all over the world?

Preheat oven to 350°.

Blend pie shell ingredients well, press into 9-inch pie plate. Bake 8 to 10 minutes, until lightly browned. Reduce oven setting to 250°.

Mix filling ingredients thoroughly, pour into pre-baked pie shell; bake at 250° for 5 minutes. Remove from oven. Reset oven to 350°.

Whip egg whites and sugar until stiff peaks form. Spread meringue on pre-baked pie, working from outside rim to center to ensure that meringue seals to pie plate. Bake at 350° for 3 to 5 minutes, until the meringue is golden brown. Chill thoroughly before serving.

Photo, plate 21
Key Lime Pie
Crumb Pie Shell
2 cups graham cracker crumbs
¼ pound butter
2 tablespoons sugar
For filling:
2 whole eggs
4 egg yolks
*1 14-ounce can sweetened
  condensed milk*
*½ cup Key lime juice (add
  more for a tarter filling)*
For meringue:
4 egg whites
*2 tablespoons confectioners'
  sugar*

Grouper La Concha

Grouper La Concha

4 pounds grouper fillets

Flour, for dredging

Vegetable oil, for frying

2 pounds mushrooms, sliced

4 tablespoons butter

1 quart heavy cream

4 scallions, sliced

2 pounds baby shrimp, shelled

1 cup rum

Salt, pepper and fresh minced garlic to taste

Lemon slices, for garnish

GROUPER LA CONCHA
Serves 6 to 8

Wash grouper fillets; while still wet, dredge in flour. Fry in oil for 10 minutes or until done, depending on the thickness of the fillets (fillets will be fork tender and easily flake, but not be dry).

While fillets cook, use a separate pan to saute mushrooms in butter until tender. Add remaining ingredients. Allow sauce to simmer, reducing by ½ to a thick consistency.

Arrange grouper fillets on a platter. Spoon the sauce over the fillets, serve with lemon garnish.

Conch Chowder

Conch Chowder

1 pound bacon

4 large green bell peppers, diced

2 large onions, diced

2 cups celery, diced

1 cup carrots, diced

2 cups potatoes, skin on, diced

2 16-ounce cans whole tomatoes

3 bay leaves

1 tablespoon oregano

3 tablespoons fresh garlic, minced

1 teaspoon cayenne pepper

1 teaspoon black pepper

½ cup white vinegar

4 tablespoons Tabasco

2 tablespoons Worcestershire

½ pound ground conch*

*Should conch be unavailable, ground abalone or giant clams are acceptable substitutes.

CONCH CHOWDER
Serves 6 to 8

A conch is a saltwater mollusk found in the tropical waters off Key West, its pink shell prized by collectors the world over. In days past, islanders saved the biggest shells for use as horn blowing instruments. Today, this tradition is kept alive by Key Westers, who hold annual conch blowing contests during the "Old Island Days" celebration.

Saute the bacon lightly in a Dutch oven or deep skillet over medium high heat. Add peppers, onions, celery, carrots and potatoes, saute an additional few minutes. Add the remaining ingredients, except for conch. Stir well, add conch.

Bring to a boil, lower heat to simmer and cook for 1 hour, adding water as necessary if chowder over-thickens.

CONCH FRITTERS
Yield, 24 fritters

In a large bowl, mix all ingredients until well blended; mixture should be of a bread dough consistency, not too moist. If needed, add extra flour in small amounts to firm.

Heat oil to 350°. Drop batter into oil in tablespoon-sized amounts (oversized fritters will not cook properly). Do not over-crowd.

Cook in small batches for 6 to 8 minutes, until golden brown.

P.S. The cook always samples the first fritter!

Conch Fritters
1 pound ground conch*
1½ cups all-purpose flour
2 eggs
1 medium green bell pepper, diced
1 medium red bell pepper, diced
1 medium onion, diced
1 tablespoon Tabasco
1 tablespoon fresh garlic, minced
Pinch cayenne pepper
Pinch ground black pepper
1 teaspoon sweet basil leaves
¼ teaspoon oregano
1½ tablespoons Old Bay seasoning
Juice of 1 fresh lemon
Salt to taste
Oil for deep-frying (peanut oil is recommended)
*Should conch be unavailable, ground abalone or giant clams are acceptable substitutes.

La Concha

La Fonda

SANTA FE, NEW MEXICO

Since before its founding in 1610, Santa Fe has had a *fonda* to accommodate travelers. Two centuries later, the adobe U.S. Hotel occupied a site on the plaza, literally at the end of the Santa Fe Trail. It quartered Confederate troops during the Civil War. Razed in 1919, the hotel was replaced in 1920 by today's La Fonda. A fine example of old Spanish Pueblo design and construction, the hotel is filled with unusual paintings and colorful, hand-decorated wooden furniture, beams and ceiling corbels, the work of local Indian and Hispanic artists. From Kit Carson to Errol Flynn to John F. Kennedy, the hotel has seen many celebrities, including many current film crews and stars.

Photo, plate 22

New Mexican Flan

2 cups sugar

3½ cups milk

¼ cup Kahlua

1 cinnamon stick

½ teaspoon nutmeg

6 eggs

1 teaspoon vanilla extract

Sliced fresh fruit for garnish

New Mexican Flan

a special egg custard topped with a Kahlua caramel sauce

Serves 6

Most New Mexico residents claim to be addicted to green chile, a crop that is well adapted to the state's bright sun and dry climate. There is virtually no food that can't be modified to incude chile, and it may be expected in local dishes at every meal. After a delicious and picante *(spicy) meal of green chile, taste buds need the cooling, soothing powers of this traditional* postre *(dessert).*

Place 1 cup sugar in heavy pan; stir over low heat until it liquifies and turns a light golden brown. Pour caramelized sugar evenly into 6 warm custard cups, set cups aside.

Preheat oven to 350°.

Put milk, Kahlua, cinnamon stick and nutmeg in a medium saucepan; scald milk over medium heat, cool. Beat eggs until foamy; slowly incorporate balance of sugar, beating well. Slowly add scalded milk to egg mixture, stirring until sugar dissolves; add vanilla.

Pour custard mixture into caramel lined cups. Place cups in a pan of hot water, bake for 1 hour and 10 minutes. To serve, invert custard cup on serving plate to dislodge, garnish with sliced fresh fruit.

PÂTÉ TOMÁS

chicken livers, cognac, butter, sherry and spices with a healthy dose of green chile

Yield, 5 cups

For years, chefs have been adapting recipes from other cultures to suit New Mexicans' craving for green chile. This recipe is the result of a happy accident that occured when a pot of hatch (New Mexico's green chile) spilled into an almost-completed vat of pâté.

Preheat oven to 400°.

Melt 3 tablespoons butter in large ovenproof skillet over medium heat. Add onions, rosemary, salt, pepper, thyme, basil, nutmeg, garlic and green chiles. Saute until onion is soft, about 10 minutes.

Add livers to skillet, saute until browned. Transfer skillet to oven, bake 5 to 8 minutes until livers are heated through. Remove from oven, cool completely.

Mix butter in food processor until light and fluffy. Add liver mixture, eggs, cognac and sherry, puree until smooth. Transfer to serving dishes or crocks, chill until firm (2 hours or overnight).

Pâté Tomás

3 tablespoons unsalted butter
2 small white onions, chopped
1 teaspoon dried rosemary
1½ teaspoons salt
1½ teaspoons white pepper, fresh ground
1 teaspoon thyme
½ teaspoon dried basil
½ teaspoon nutmeg
1 teaspoon garlic, minced
½ cup green chiles, chopped
1 pound chicken livers, washed, trimmed, patted dry
1¾ cups (3½ sticks) unsalted butter at room temperature
2 hard boiled eggs
2 tablespoons cognac
2 tablespoons dry sherry

SOUR CREAM CHICKEN ENCHILADAS

chunks of chicken, green chiles, onions and spices, folded in a blue corn tortilla, smothered with green chile sauce and topped with a generous dollop of sour cream

Serves 4 to 6

The French make crepes, the Italians make manicotti ... New Mexicans make enchiladas. As long as people have been eating, they have been wrapping cheese and other morsels to create tube-shaped treats. The early settlers of New Mexico no doubt combined the traditional tortillas with chile and meat for an early version of an enchilada.

In large pot, place whole chicken with enough water to cover. Cover and simmer until chicken is done, about 1 hour. Remove chicken, retain broth; Remove meat from chicken, discard bones and skin.

Add flour to broth, cook 5 minutes, until slightly thickened. Add garlic, chiles, chicken meat, bouillon cubes, simmer for 20 to 25 minutes.

Lightly fry tortillas in oil, drain. Place a small amount of sauce on dish, top with tortilla, more sauce, cheese, onion and dollops of sour cream. Repeat process to desired stack, 2 to 3 is adequate. Heat in 350° oven until cheese is melted. Garnish with dollop of sour cream, shredded lettuce and tomatoes.

Sour Cream Chicken Enchiladas

For chicken sauce:
1 3-pound chicken
Water to cover
4 to 6 tablespoons of flour
4 cloves garlic, finely chopped
2 cups hot green chiles, diced
4 chicken bouillon cubes
For enchiladas:
1 dozen blue corn tortillas
Oil for frying
8 ounces cheddar cheese, shredded
1 medium onion, chopped
2 cups sour cream
1 head lettuce, shredded
2 tomatoes, diced

Black Bean Soup

⅛ cup olive oil

⅛ pound bacon, diced

⅛ pound smoked ham,
  cut in 2-inch pieces

2 medium onions, chopped

2 cloves garlic, minced

2 stalks celery, chopped

1½ cups dried black beans

2½ teaspoons dried ground
  red chile

4 cups water

Salt and pepper to taste

¼ cup sherry

⅛ cup white vinegar

1 tablespoon instant beef
  bouillon

1 teaspoon chopped cilantro,
  for garnish

New Mexican Chorizo Burrito

8 eggs

4 tablespoons milk or water

4 to 8 teaspoons butter or
  margarine

¼ cup white onion, diced

¼ cup green chile, diced

2 cups shredded Monterey Jack
  or cheddar cheese

4 flour tortillas

Salt and pepper to taste

8 2-ounce pieces of chorizo

Southwestern Artichoke Dip

½ cup mayonnaise

½ cup sour cream

½ cup green chile, drained
  and chopped

1 15-ounce can artichoke hearts,
  drained and chopped

½ cup grated parmesan cheese

Tabasco and Worcestershire
  to taste

Salt and pepper to taste

6 fresh artichokes

Blue corn tostadas

SANTA FE BLACK BEAN SOUP

*frijoles negros are blended with bacon, ham and green chile for a delicious
spicy and pureed soup—a great party favorite*

Serves 6 to 8

*Over a thousand years ago, ancient Indian tribes living in New Mexico
grew staples of corn and beans. When the Spaniards arrived in the area in the
late 16th century, pork and chile were added to the local diet and have remained
part of the traditional cuisine.*

In large pan, heat oil; add bacon, ham, onions, garlic and celery, brown
until vegetables are soft, about 40 minutes.

Clean beans, drain and add to pan with dried chile pepper, water and
instant bouillon. Bring to boil, reduce heat, cover and simmer until beans
are tender, 2½ to 3 hours. Skim fat occasionally from top of soup.

Use food processor or blender to puree mixture until smooth. Refrigerate
overnight. Reheat at serving time, test seasonings, salt and pepper to taste.
Stir in sherry and vinegar just prior to serving. Garnish with chopped
cilantro.

NEW MEXICAN CHORIZO BURRITO

Serves 4

Prepare Red or Green Chili Sauce (page 119) and set aside.

In a bowl, beat eggs and milk or water until blended. Heat a large pan,
add butter or margarine. Saute onion and chile until tender. Add egg mixture
to pan and mix together until eggs are scrambled.

Peel chorizo. Cook in pan until done. Drain fat, add chorizo to egg mixture
and mix together. Heat flour tortilla. Divide egg mixture into 4 parts and
roll each into a flour tortilla. Place on a plate, pour chili sauce over burrito.
Sprinkle cheese on top and place in oven long enough for cheese to melt.

SOUTHWESTERN ARTICHOKE DIP

Serves 4 to 6

In a large bowl, combine mayonnaise, sour cream, green chile, chopped
artichoke hearts, parmesan cheese, Tabasco, Worcestershire, salt and pepper.

Take fresh artichokes and cook. When done, carve out the middle and
stuff it with the artichoke dip. Serve surrounded by blue corn tostadas.

La Playa Hotel

Built as a stylish rockwork mansion in 1904 by Norwegian-born artist Chris Jorgensen for his bride, a daughter of the Ghirardelli family of San Francisco, La Playa was converted into a hotel in 1916. Restoration and renovation were completed in 1984. The residential feel of the hotel's Mediterranean design is highlighted by pale pink stuccoed walls, red-tile roofs, and a lobby featuring a large marble fireplace, European antiques and hand-loomed rugs. Distinctively appointed guest rooms—with views of either the ocean, exquisite formal gardens and landscaped patios or residential Carmel—feature unique hand-carved furnishings incorporating the hotel's mermaid motif.

SALMON OVER LENTILS AND FRESH VEGETABLES
Serves 4

California's central coast is where the sea meets fertile fields of produce. The following recipes celebrate La Playa's auspicious location by bringing together the best of marine flavors with those grown from the soil.

Heat lentils and chicken stock to boiling, cover and simmer until lentils are tender, about 30 minutes. Add more stock during cooking, if necessary.

Melt butter in large saute pan. Add vegetables, herbs, garlic, shallot and ham, cook until all are tender and flavors mixed. Add the cooked lentils and a little butter (you may wish to moisten the mixture with a little white wine or chicken stock).

In saucepan, reduce white wine to ¼ cup; add the cream, reduce by same amount. Bit by bit, whisk butter until you have a smooth sauce.

Saute the salmon fillets in butter until cooked to your liking.

To serve, spoon the sauce onto 4 warmed serving plates, place lentil mixture in the center of the plate and salmon over the lentils.

Photo, plate 23
Salmon over Lentils and Fresh Vegetables
1 cup dry lentils
2 cups chicken stock
2 tablespoons butter
1 leek, finely chopped
1 carrot, finely chopped
1 zucchini, finely chopped
1 yellow squash, finely chopped
1 handful chives, chopped
1 handful parsley, chopped
1 tablespoon garlic, chopped
1 tablespoon shallot, chopped
1 handful prosciutto ham,
  thinly slivered
1 cup white wine
¼ cup heavy cream
1 cup butter
4 salmon fillets
Butter for sauteing

Warm Lobster Salad

For each serving:

½ cup fresh vegetables of choice,
  cut to serving size
2 tablespoons olive oil
2 to 3 ounces assorted fresh
  wild mushrooms (shiitake,
  chanterelle, etc.)
1 tablespoon fennel and
  coriander seeds, freshly crushed
Salt and pepper
2 to 3 ounces lobster meat,
  removed from shell
½ medium tomato, peeled,
  seeded and diced,
  juices reserved
Brandy
Lettuce

Seared Rare Yellowfin Tuna

For marinade, blend:

¼ cup sesame oil
¼ cup soy sauce
¼ cup wine
¼ cup balsamic vinegar
1 tablespoon powdered ginger
1 12-ounce loin-shaped cut of
  top-quality yellowfin tuna
3 tablespoons sesame oil
4 artichoke hearts

Citrus Dressing

1½ cups extra virgin olive oil
Juice of 1 grapefruit
3 cups orange juice, reduced
  to 1 cup
Salt and pepper
3 tablespoons chopped chives

WARM LOBSTER AND WILD MUSHROOM SALAD

Blanch vegetables by immersing in boiling water until done to the firmness you prefer. Drain and reserve.

Heat olive oil in large saute pan, add mushrooms and crushed seeds, season with salt and pepper. Saute a few moments to dissipate water content and concentrate flavors. Add lobster and tomatoes, cook for about 45 seconds, then add a healthy splash of good brandy and the reserved tomato juices. Allow alcohol to burn away, remove from heat (it's important not to toughen the lobster by overcooking).

While the lobster cooks, rewarm vegetables in their cooking water, drain.

To serve, cover plate with a small amount of lettuce. Arrange vegetables attractively on the lettuce to create a nest in the center, spoon the hot lobster mixture into the nest. Pour the pan juices over the salad as a dressing.

SEARED RARE YELLOWFIN TUNA OVER ARTICHOKES

Serves 4

Marinate tuna for 4 hours, turning occasionally.

Heat a large skillet to very hot. Add sesame oil and marinated tuna; sear 1 side, cook for 2 minutes. Repeat process on all sides of fish (the tuna should remain raw in the center). Remove from heat, allow to rest at room temperature.

For dressing, whisk olive oil into mixture of grapefruit juice and reduced orange juice. Season with salt, pepper and chopped chives.

Place artichoke hearts in centers of 4 plates. Slice the tuna and place a portion on each artichoke, spoon dressing around and over.

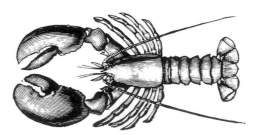

SEA BASS IN TOMATO-FENNEL FONDUE
Serves 4

Saute fennel, shallots and garlic gently in olive oil until slightly softened; add ½ of the crushed fennel and coriander seeds. Add tomato paste, cook for 1 minute or more, add chopped tomatoes and juices and white wine. Simmer gently for 20 to 30 minutes to a favorable consistency; season with salt and pepper, reserve.

Mix chopped parsley and remaining seeds. Season fillets with salt and pepper, sprinkle lightly with olive oil, coat tops of fillets with parsley mixture. Saute fillets, coated side down, in 2 tablespoons olive oil for about 2 minutes; turn and finish cooking.

Reheat fondue, spoon onto warmed serving plates. Place fillets on fondue, coated side up. Garnish with olives.

EGGPLANT MOUSSE
with fresh vegetables and feta cheese
Serves 4

Preheat oven to 350˚.

Cut eggplants in half lengthwise and score by cutting deep slits with a knife; rub each face with 1 tablespoon of the olive oil. Roast eggplants until the pulp is thoroughly softened (browning is fine), cool.

Scrape eggplant pulp into a food processor; add all ingredients except olive oil, blend until homogenous. While still mixing, add olive oil in a thin stream until it is incorporated and the mixture is smooth; adjust seasonings.

Sea Bass in
Tomato-Fennel Fondue
1 bulb fennel, finely chopped
4 shallots, finely chopped
3 cloves garlic, finely chopped
2 tablespoons olive oil
2 tablespoons fennel seeds,
* crushed*
2 tablespoons coriander seeds,
* crushed*
2 tablespoons tomato paste
4 large ripe tomatoes, seeded,
* chopped, juice reserved*
1 cup white wine
Salt and pepper
The sea bass:
1 bunch parsley, washed,
* chopped, wrung dry*
4 sea bass fillets
Salt and pepper
Olive oil
Black olives for garnish

Eggplant Mousse
2 eggplants
1¼ cups extra virgin olive oil
2 egg yolks
1 cup fresh oregano
2 cups fresh basil
3 tablespoons garlic, chopped
Salt and pepper
Feta cheese
Fresh vegetables of your choice
Croutons (optional)

La Playa Hotel

Martha Washington Inn

ABINGDON, VIRGINIA

Tucked away in the Southern Highlands of Virginia is the award-winning Martha Washington Inn, constructed in 1832 as a residence for the large family of Colonel Francis Preston and his wife, Sara. The building has served as a women's college as well as a Civil War hospital. In 1935, "The Martha" opened as one of Virginia's finest hotels. The four historic buildings comprising the inn were painstakingly restored to their original Victorian elegance in 1985 at the cost of more than $8 million. Offering every amenity —including ghost stories—The Martha's staff is dedicated to fine service and personal attention.

TROUT SOUTHERN TRADITION
Serves 4

In the southwestern region of Virginia, run-off from the Blue Ridge Mountains feeds sparkling streams and rivers. These waterways are home to an abundance of marine life. Freshwater crabs and crawfish burrow in the silted banks, while striped bass, bluegill, catfish, perch and trout patrol the narrows. Of these, the trout has achieved status as among the most enjoyed components of Southern cookery.

The combination of bourbon whiskey, trout, cornmeal and vegetables is a reflection of the variety of foods which make up the taste of southwestern Virginia, the "mountain empire."

Remove heads from fish, if desired, and trim all fins. Rinse in cold water briefly and place in refrigerator.

Heat butter in saute pan. Add all stuffing ingredients except cheese and crabmeat. Saute for 5 minutes or until celery is just cooked. Remove from heat and stir to cool. When at room temperature, add the grated cheese and lump crabmeat to the mixture; set aside.

Divide the stuffing among the trout and fill each fish. Press the fish together firmly to eliminate air pockets in the filling.

Preheat oven to 325°.

Dredge the fish in the cornmeal. In a large skillet heat the oil. Add the fish and lightly brown. Turn the fish over and cook an additional 2

Photo, plate 24

Trout Southern Tradition

4 rainbow trout, deboned and butterflied
½ cup yellow cornmeal
¼ cup peanut oil
2 cups mushrooms, sliced
¼ cup bourbon
¼ cup Southern Comfort
2 cups heavy cream
2 teaspoons Lea and Perrins White Wine Worcestershire
2 tablespoons cold butter, cut into pieces

Crabmeat Stuffing

1 tablespoon clarified butter
¼ cup celery, chopped
⅓ cup green onions, sliced
¼ cup bell pepper, chopped
½ teaspoon garlic, minced
1 teaspoon fresh thyme
1 teaspoon fresh tarragon
Salt and pepper to taste
⅓ cup grated white cheddar cheese
6 ounces Virginia lump crab

minutes. Place on an oven-proof platter, bake for 12 to 15 minutes.

Meanwhile, drain all but 1 teaspoon oil from the pan, add mushrooms and saute 3 minutes. Carefully add the bourbon and Southern Comfort to the pan (this will flame, so be cautious), allow the pan juices to reduce to ¼ cup. Add the cream and White Wine Worcestershire sauce, reduce until slightly thickened.

Remove the pan from the heat. Add the butter piece by piece, shaking the pan to incorporate it. When ready, remove fish to serving platter and bathe lightly with the cream sauce.

Roasted Quail Regent
Serves 4

In a shallow non-metallic pan, combine wine with oils and fresh herbs. Lay quails in the mixture and cover. Allow to marinate 30 minutes; turn, marinate an additional 15 minutes.

Preheat oven to 350°.

Combine bread cubes, egg, stock and apples; carefully fold in cooked rice and herbs. Stuff quails, tucking legs into the body cavity cross-wise to seal in the stuffing; fold wings under and lock in place. Wrap a piece of bacon around each bird and place on a roasting rack. Lightly season quails with salt and pepper. Roast until quails are tender, about 30 minutes.

Prepare sauce in a heavy-walled pan over medium flame, reducing vermouth and port wine with onions to ⅓ of its original volume. Remove onions, add chicken stock; reduce to about ¾ cup. Add heavy cream, reduce until thickened. Add tomato paste, whisking lightly. Remove any fat from the roasting pan, whisk remaining juices into the sauce, allow to thicken again.

To serve, divide birds equally between 4 serving plates, coat lightly with the sauce.

Roasted Quail Regent
1 cup Virginia Reisling wine
¼ cup olive oil
¼ cup peanut oil
½ cup fresh herbs, minced
  (we like lemon thyme,
  apple sage and rosemary)
8 European-style,
  semi-boneless quails
At preparation:
8 strips lean bacon
Salt and pepper
For stuffing:
4 cups day-old French bread,
  cubed
1 egg, beaten
½ cup chicken or veal stock, cool
1 small Granny Smith apple,
  pared, cored and diced
½ cup cooked blended rice
Parsley, thyme and sage,
  to taste, chopped
Regent Sauce
1¾ cups dry vermouth
½ cup port wine
¼ cup green onions, chopped
¼ cup chicken stock
1 ½ cups heavy cream
1 teaspoon tomato paste

Martha Washington Inn

Scampi Morocco

Scampi Morocco

20 medium shrimp, peeled and deveined, tail on

2 tablespoons clarified butter

1 cup sauterne

2 to 3 cloves fresh garlic, minced

1 tablespoon fresh thyme

1 tablespoon fresh basil, minced

Juice of 1 lemon

1 tablespoon fresh parsley, minced

6 tablespoons cold butter, cut into small cubes

2 tomatoes, peeled, seeded and diced

1 tablespoon lemon zest, grated

4 cups fresh spinach, trimmed and washed

¼ cup feta or other briny cheese

SCAMPI MOROCCO

Serves 4

Saute shrimp in clarified butter for 1 minute on each side. Add wine, garlic, thyme, basil, lemon juice and parsley; reduce liquid slightly. Remove pan from heat, add butter piece-by-piece by shaking the pan until all butter is incorporated. Add diced tomatoes and zest.

Meanwhile, quickly wilt spinach in a steamer or microwave to bring out the emerald color. Place wilted spinach on plates, arrange shrimp on top. Distribute pan sauce evenly and top with crumbled feta cheese.

Hot Fudge Cake

Hot Fudge Cake

1 pound butter, softened

3 cups granulated sugar

14 whole eggs

3½ cups all-purpose flour

2½ teaspoons baking powder

1 teaspoon salt

2 cups chocolate syrup

1 teaspoon vanilla extract

AUDREY'S HOT FUDGE CAKE

Yield, 1 8-inch by 13-inch cake

Preheat oven to 350°.

Cream butter and sugar, add eggs and blend well. Add all dry ingredients, ensuring all are thoroughly incorporated. Add remaining ingredients, stir until smooth.

Spray baking pan with spray pan coating and lightly flour. Pour batter into the pan, tapping edges to release air bubbles. Bake until center is almost set (about 35 minutes). The cake will be very moist.

Serve warm with Hot Fudge Sauce (page 122).

Bourbon Pecan Pie

Bourbon Pecan Pie

5 eggs

1 cup packed brown sugar

¼ teaspoon salt

½ cup corn syrup

3 tablespoons butter, melted and cooled

3 tablespoons bourbon

½ teaspoon vanilla extract

2½ cups pecans, chopped

Unbaked pastry shell

BOURBON PECAN PIE

Yield, 1 8-inch pie

Preheat oven to 325°.

Put eggs in a mixing bowl and beat; blend in sugar, salt and corn syrup. Stir in butter, bourbon and vanilla, mixing until thoroughly blended. Add the chopped pecans.

Pour mixture into an unbaked pastry shell. Bake until filling is set, approximately 25 to 35 minutes.

The Mayflower—A Stouffer Hotel

WASHINGTON, D.C.

A true "inaugural address," The Mayflower's tradition of service dates back to the 1925 Coolidge Inauguration when 1,000 people attended the hotel's grand opening. When The Mayflower opened its doors, it boasted more gold leaf than any building in the country and was one of the capital's first air-conditioned hotels. The recent $70 million restoration is spectacular: over 56 miles of millwork were used for crown moldings; 46,000 square feet of Italian marble were hand-set in the baths. Rediscovered was a 60 x 25-foot skylight blacked-out at the beginning of World War II. Also uncovered were two large murals by the famous artist Edward Lanning.

❧

COLD POACHED SHRIMP AND SCALLOPS
with marinated asparagus
Serves 4

The Mayflower has hosted every president since its opening in 1925, and has offered each a vast array of seafood delicacies from regional waters. This hotel specialty, featured today in the hotel's Cafe Promenade, combines subtle seasonings to bring out the best of the delicate flavors of shrimp and scallops.

Cut woody stems off asparagus; place asparagus in a large amount of boiling salt water. Boil uncovered for about 3 minutes, chill completely in ice water, drain and set aside.

For Fish Stock, combine ingredients and bring to a light simmer. Cook 20 to 30 minutes, skim and strain. Combine wine, Fish Stock and basil stems, bring to a boil. Add scallops and shrimp, boil 3 minutes then cover and remove from heat. Let seafood stand in hot liquid for about 5 minutes until it is cooked. Remove from liquid and let cool.

Reduce seafood liquid by boiling until ¼ to ⅓ cup remains. Dissolve cornstarch in water, whisk into boiling liquid bit by bit to let thicken slightly, strain and cool. To create marinade, add vinegar, olive oil, chopped basil, salt and pepper to the cooled liquid and whip well.

Slice scallops, peel and devein shrimp. Arrange asparagus and seafood on chilled plate. Drizzle with marinade, sprinkle with chopped tomato.

Photo, plate 25
Poached Shrimp and Scallops
20 asparagus spears
¾ cup Fish Stock
¾ cup white wine
Basil stems
6 ounces sea scallops
12 large (16/20 count) shrimp, shell on
2 tablespoons cornstarch
2 tablespoons water
2 tablespoons cider vinegar
2 tablespoons olive oil
½ tablespoon fresh basil, chopped
Salt and pepper to taste
1 tomato, seeded, diced small
Fish Stock
½ cup white wine
½ cup water
1 pound fish bones
2 tablespoons shallots, chopped
2 tablespoons celery, chopped
2 tablespoons leeks, chopped

Charred Tuna Pepper Steak

2 tablespoons olive oil

2 tablespoons teriyaki sauce

1 teaspoon honey

1 teaspoon soy sauce

2 7-ounce pieces Ahi tuna

2 pieces endive, julienne

1 tablespoon lime juice

1 pinch sugar

Salt and pepper to taste

Black Bean Ginger Sauce

½ cup black beans*

1 cup chicken stock

½ ounce ginger root, peeled,
  finely julienne

2 tablespoons cracked black
  peppercorns

Butter for sauteing

*Soak dry beans in water for 12
  hours, then cook in chicken
  stock until tender.

Tomato Soup

2 pounds tomatoes

¼ cup olive oil

3 tablespoons garlic,
  finely chopped

1 teaspoon basil, chopped

Salt and pepper

3 tablespoons black
  mustard seeds

3 tablespoons fresh ginger, finely
  chopped

3 tablespoons curry leaves,
  julienne

Pinch white pepper

¼ cup plain yogurt

CHARRED TUNA PEPPER STEAK
marinated tuna with endives and Black Bean Ginger Sauce
Serves 2

Blend olive oil, teriyaki sauce, honey and soy sauce, marinate the tuna in the mixture for 2 hours. Saute the endives quickly in a pan with lime juice and sugar. Salt and pepper to taste, set aside.

Puree ½ of the black beans. Add chicken stock to the puree, blend until smooth.

Blanch julienne of ginger in water for a few minutes.

Remove tuna from the marinade. Rub cracked peppercorn on each side. In a small amount of butter, saute 3 minutes on each side, until cooked medium. Remove tuna and deglaze pan with the marinade; add black bean sauce, stir to blend.

To serve, place endives in the center of the plate and pool black bean sauce, then top with ginger. Place tuna on top of sauce and garnish with remainder of black beans.

TOMATO SOUP
with black mustard seed and curry leaves
Serves 4

Cut up tomatoes and saute in ⅛ cup olive oil with garlic and basil, salt and pepper to taste. Puree sauteed tomatoes in food processor.

In a pan, heat ⅛ cup olive oil until very hot. Add mustard seeds and saute until they crack. Add ginger, saute for a few minutes. Add curry leaves and let "frizzle"; add white pepper. Add the pureed tomatoes to the pan, season to taste.

Serve topped with yogurt.

Photography: Hunt Commercial Photography

COLOR PLATE 17
Supreme Chocolate Almond Torte, page 49
The Hotel Hershey, Hershey, Pennsylvania

Photography: Jonathan Sherrill & Richard Carpenter

COLOR PLATE 18

Indian Pudding, page 52
Hotel Northampton, Northampton, Massachusetts

Photography: Kanji Takeno

COLOR PLATE 19
Roast Pheasant Stuffed with Oysters and Ham, page 55
The Jefferson Sheraton, Richmond, Virginia

Photography: Terry Richardson

COLOR PLATE 20
Rutledge House Inn's She-Crab Soup, page 58
John Rutledge House Inn, Charleston, South Carolina

Photography: Florida Keys Magazine

COLOR PLATE 21
Key Lime Pie, page 61
La Concha — A Holiday Inn Hotel, Key West, Florida

Photography: Carolyn Wright

COLOR PLATE 22

New Mexican Flan, page 64

La Fonda, Santa Fe, New Mexico

Photography: Grant Huntington

COLOR PLATE 23
Salmon over Lentils and Fresh Vegetables, page 67
La Playa Hotel, Carmel, California

Photography: Tim C. Cox

COLOR PLATE 24
Trout Southern Tradition, page 70
Martha Washington Inn, Abingdon, Virginia

Seared Medallions of Salmon
with pesto, red bell pepper coulis and sun-dried tomatoes
Serves 4

Roast bell pepper in 350° oven for 5 minutes; peel, remove seeds and stem. Place in a blender, add chicken stock, blend to a coulis consistency. Keep warm.

To make pesto, combine finely chopped garlic, basil, parsley and pine nuts with olive oil. Season with salt and pepper.

Sear medallions of salmon 1 minute on each side. Place pesto on top. Bake slowly in oven at 325° for 8 minutes.

To serve, pool red bell pepper puree on plate. Arrange salmon on sauce and garnish with julienne sun-dried tomatoes.

Medallions of Salmon
1 large red bell pepper
½ cup chicken stock
3 garlic cloves, finely chopped
1 bunch basil, finely chopped
½ bunch parsley, finely chopped
⅓ cup pine nuts, finely chopped
3 tablespoons olive oil
Salt and pepper to taste
4 4-ounce salmon fillets
4 pieces sun-dried tomatoes,
 julienne

Rum Pecan Crème Brûlée
Serves 6

In a bowl, mix sugar, egg yolks and egg.

Bring heavy cream to a boil, add to the sugar and egg mixture. Let it stand off heat for 10 minutes, add rum.

Cook sugar and water in a copper pan until it caramelizes. Then pour it into small round ceramic molds and sprinkle pecans on top, add cream and egg mixture.

Preheat oven to 300°.

Place the molds in a water bath, bake for 45 minutes. When almost done, sprinkle some sugar on top of each crème brûlée. Just prior to serving, brown under a broiler.

This crème brûlée may be served warm or cold.

Rum Pecan Crème Brûlée
⅓ cup sugar
3 egg yolks
1 whole egg
1 cup heavy cream
2 tablespoons rum
⅓ cup sugar
1 tablespoon water
2 tablespoons pecans

Mayflower Banana Bread
Yield, 2 loaves

Preheat oven to 350°.

Mix together sugar and butter. Slowly mix in eggs, bananas, vanilla and sour cream until smooth. Mix in remaining ingredients.

Bake in greased loaf pans for 1¼ hours.

Mayflower Banana Bread
2 cups granulated sugar
1 cup butter, softened
4 eggs
1 pound bananas, creamed
1 teaspoon vanilla extract
1 cup sour cream
1 cup cake flour
2 cups all-purpose flour
1½ teaspoons baking soda
1 teaspoon salt
½ cup pecans, chopped

The Mayflower

Menger Hotel

SAN ANTONIO, TEXAS

Located adjacent to the Alamo, the Menger Hotel was built on the site of William Menger's brewery, the first in Texas. Opening on the first of February, 1859, the hotel has been host to such notables as Sam Houston, generals Lee and Grant, and presidents Taft and McKinley. Teddy Roosevelt recruited San Antonio's Rough Riders in The Menger Bar. This handsome structure boasts original wrought-iron balconies and details. Many rooms retain the furniture, art and accessories from the hotel's earlier days, including four-poster beds, velvet-covered Victorian sofas and chairs, marble-topped tables and period wallcoverings.

Photo, plate 26

Grilled Chicken Salad

8 ounces boneless chicken breast

½ teaspoon cilantro, chopped

1 teaspoon green onion, diced

½ teaspoon fresh garlic, minced

1 teaspoon Thai peppers, minced

1½ teaspoons granulated sugar

2 tablespoons bottled oriental
   fish sauce

¼ cup cucumber, peeled, seeded
   and diced

6 slices lime

½ teaspoon fresh lime juice

Salt to taste

MENGER GRILLED CHICKEN SALAD
Serves 2

Featured in epicurean magazines, Menger Grilled Chicken Salad has consistently received rave reviews from food critics. A distinctly regional dish, it acquires its discrete Southwestern flavor by employing a blend of cilantro, lime and Thai peppers that produce a delightful salad, pleasing to the eye as well as the palate. This Southwestern dish joins other traditional menu offerings available in the hotel's historic Colonial Dining Room, the San Antonio choice of luminaries from generals Lee and Grant to presidents Roosevelt and Eisenhower.

Quickly charbroil chicken over high heat until well charred, but still moist. Do not overcook. Cool and cut in a ¼-inch dice.

In bowl, combine chicken, cilantro, green onion, garlic, Thai peppers, sugar and fish sauce. Cover and refrigerate for at least 1 hour.

Toss with cucumber, lime and lime juice. Salt to taste, serve.

BUÑUELOS WITH CHOCOLATE AND STRAWBERRY CREAM
Serves 4

The buñuelo originated from interior Mexico. It was a family's way of making use of their leftover tortillas. The leftover tortillas were pan-fried and then dusted with cinnamon and sugar, making them great treats for their children.

Sauce the base of a dinner plate with Strawberry Sauce. Place a buñuelo in center of sauced plate. Using a pastry bag or a spoon, spread Chocolate Mousse evenly, leaving ¼-inch lip on the buñuelo. Place another buñuelo on top, then spread Strawberry Mousse in the same manner. Place third buñuelo on top, spread whipped cream over. Drizzle with chocolate syrup.

Buñuelos with Cream
For each serving:
3 tablespoons Strawberry Sauce
  (page 124)
3 buñuelos
3 tablespoons Chocolate Mousse
3 tablespoons Strawberry
  Mousse
2 tablespoons whipped cream
1 tablespoon chocolate syrup

BUÑUELOS
Yield, 12 4-inch buñuelos

Brew tea; add cinnamon, nutmeg and anise. Gradually add tea mixture to flour to make a soft dough. Knead dough into a round soft ball. Form small balls out of dough (about 2 tablespoons). Let dough sit for 10 minutes.

Dust both cutting board and rolling pin with flour. Roll out dough balls paper thin and cut into a 4-inch tortilla shape. Using a fork, perforate dough before cooking.

Deep fry until crisp, turning occasionally (about 1 minute).

Buñuelos
⅓ cup hot tea
¼ teaspoon cinnamon sticks,
  crushed
¼ teaspoon nutmeg
¼ teaspoon anise
1⅓ cups all-purpose flour
Oil, for deep-frying

CHOCOLATE MOUSSE
Yield, 1½ cups

Melt chocolate on top of a double boiler.

Combine egg yolks, sugar, whipping cream and vanilla; whip to a peak. Fold in chocolate mixture.

Put mixture into freezer until it sets (approximately 15 to 20 minutes).

Chocolate Mousse
3 tablespoons semi-sweet
  chocolate chips
5 egg yolks
⅔ tablespoon sugar
¾ cup heavy whipping cream
Vanilla extract to taste

STRAWBERRY MOUSSE
Yield, 1½ cups

Whip egg yolks and sugar to a peak. Gradually add Strawberry Sauce to mixture. Whip heavy cream to a peak. Fold strawberry mixture into whipping cream.

Put mixture into freezer until it sets (approximately 15 to 20 minutes).

Strawberry Mousse
4 egg yolks
2 teaspoons sugar
½ cup plus 1 tablespoon
  Strawberry Sauce (page 124)
⅓ cup heavy cream

Menger Hotel

Escargot Colonial

Escargot Colonial

24 escargot

ESCARGOT COLONIAL
baked escargot with Green Chili Pesto
Serves 4

Preheat oven to 400°.

Place 6 escargot into each escargot dish and cover with Green Chili Pesto. Bake for approximately 8 minutes or until the pesto starts to boil. Remove from oven and serve.

Green Chili Pesto

Green Chili Pesto

¼ cup cilantro, chopped

1 tablespoon pine nuts,
 finely chopped

2 tablespoons romano cheese,
 grated

½ teaspoon ground pepper

¼ cup olive oil

1 tablespoon fresh garlic,
 chopped

GREEN CHILI PESTO
Yield, 1½ cups

This pesto's zest comes from the chopped cilantro .... "Green Chili Pesto" contains no green chile!

Combine all of the ingredients in a food processor. Puree completely.

Menger Tortilla Soup

Menger Tortilla Soup

5 ounces ground beef

¾ cup yellow onions, chopped

¼ cup Poblano peppers, chopped

½ cup Anaheim peppers,
 chopped

1¼ cups tomatoes, diced

½ cup tomato paste

3 quarts chicken stock

½ teaspoon cumin

4 sprigs cilantro

½ teaspoon granulated garlic

Black pepper to taste

Garnish, per serving:

2 tablespoons of deep-fried
 tortilla strips

1 teaspoon Monterey Jack cheese,
 grated

1 teaspoon cheddar cheese,
 grated

MENGER TORTILLA SOUP
Serves 8

Brown ground beef, drain fat. Add onions, peppers and tomatoes. Saute until just tender. Add tomato paste. Saute lightly (do not let paste burn). Add stock and seasoning. Bring to a boil, simmer for 45 minutes. Before serving, skim excess fat.

To serve, pour soup into bowls, garnish with deep-fried tortilla strips and 2 teaspoons of cheese blend.

Mohonk Mountain House

NEW PALTZ, NEW YORK

Created by twin brothers Albert and Alfred Smiley, Quaker schoolteachers, the Mountain House opened in 1870 as a 40-room summer retreat. Nestled in the Shawangunk Mountains at the head of a quarter-mile glacial lake, it is surrounded by thousands of acres of wilderness, formal gardens and riding and hiking trails. The resort was sensitively enlarged over its first 30 years to include 276 guest rooms, three dining rooms and two formal parlors. A National Historic Landmark, the hotel is an assimilation of fanciful turreted and crenelated local-stone and gabled-frame constructions spanning the late Victorian Revival through the Arts and Crafts periods of American architectural design.

❧

MOHONK GRIDDLE CAKES
Yield, 8 to 10 cakes

The history of the pancake (griddle cake) spans several centuries and belongs to all grain-growing countries. Olney, England has held a Pancake Race annually on Shrove Tuesday for several hundred years. Germany has its enormous "table top" pancake, Israel its "blintzes," Sweden its "plattar," France its "crepes," the Russians "sirniki" and the Dutch "flenjses." The original pancake in America was called the "Johnny Hoe-Cake."

An old Mohonk tale relates the humor of Mr. Francis Smiley. Reportedly, he would come into the kitchen and tell a new cook the only way one could tell if the griddle batter was just right was to "count the bubbles." This futile task was similar to sending the cook out for a bucket of steam.

In mixing bowl, blend eggs and sugar with a whisk; add ⅔ of the milk. When well mixed, add all dry ingredients; incorporate balance of milk slowly, scraping bowl the whole time. Add vanilla and butter slowly, mix until smooth (do not beat, or cakes will be tough). Batter is better if allowed to rest overnight. Bake on hot griddle, turn only once.

Note: For variety, incorporate blueberries, raspberries, strawberries, huckleberries, etc.

Photo, plate 27
Mohonk Griddle Cakes
2 eggs
2 tablespoons sugar
1½ cups milk
1¼ cups bread flour
1¼ cups cake flour
1 teaspoon baking powder
Pinch salt
Vanilla extract to taste
⅛ cup butter, melted and slightly cooled

Cooking for a club or social group?
Yield, about 285 griddle cakes
2 quarts eggs
2½ pounds sugar
1½ gallons milk
5 pounds bread flour
5 pounds cake flour
10 ounces baking powder
2 tablespoons salt, or just a pinch if using salted butter
Vanilla extract to taste
2 pounds butter, melted and slightly cooled

Sole Marie

Sole Marie

For each serving:

1 4- to 5-ounce fresh sole fillet, skinless

Salt and white pepper

¼ fresh pear (without seeds), sliced and fanned

¼ cup Swiss Altime pear-flavored mineral water or unsweetened pear nectar

1½ tablespoons dry white wine or dry vermouth

¼ cup evaporated skim milk

Fresh dill, for garnish

SOLE MARIE
a Sound Choice selection

Healthful eating and creative recreation are a popular combination for today's traveler. To satisfy their guests, the Mohonk Mountain House created the Sound Choice Menu to provide food items that are good for the body and pleasing to the palate. The recipes are reduced in fat, cholesterol, calories and sodium. Sole Marie is just one example.

Preheat oven to 375°

Lightly season skin side of fillet with salt and pepper, fold ends under with skin side down, place in an oven-safe saute pan that has been sprayed with vegetable oil. Place fanned pear on top, add mineral water and wine. Cover with foil and cook until tender, 10 to 12 minutes.

Remove fish to a warmed plate with a slotted spatula, allowing juices to drip back into the pan. Add evaporated skim milk to juices, reduce to desired consistency over medium heat, stirring occasionally.

When reduced, pour over fish, or serve on the side. Garnish with sprig of fresh dill.

Roasted Eggplant

Roasted Eggplant

3 large eggplants, peeled, sliced ¼-inch thick, cut into 1-inch strips

2 ripe tomatoes, ¼-inch diced

1 medium red onion, ¼-inch diced

1 bunch fresh chives, chopped

4 spring onions, chopped

2 cloves garlic, fine diced

1 bunch fresh oregano, chopped

1 bunch fresh basil, chopped

¼ cup romano cheese, grated

⅛ cup canola oil

⅛ cup olive oil

¼ cup balsamic vinegar

To Serve:

Lettuce

Red bell pepper, roasted and julienne, for garnish

ROASTED EGGPLANT IN ITALIAN VINAIGRETTE
Serves 12

Combine all ingredients, let marinate for 1 hour.

Preheat oven to 375°.

Spread mixture on a roasting pan and bake for 20 minutes; chill. Serve on a bed of lettuce with roasted red pepper garnish.

Cheese and Parsley Sausage
Serves 10

This unusual, incredibly tasty sausage may be cooked as is, or for the ambitious country-at-heart, stuffed in natural casings.

Grind pork through a large meat grinder die, or use food processor to rough chop; place in a large bowl. Combine salt, pepper and fennel seeds, add to meat, blend thoroughly. Add cheese and parsley, using water to bind ingredients.

The sausage mixture may be cooked as patties or stuffed in natural casings. Roast or broil until internal temperature is at least 140°. Serve with risotto or pasta.

Cheese and Parsley Sausage
5 pounds pork butt, 1-inch cubed
1 tablespoon salt
1 tablespoon course ground black pepper
1 tablespoon fennel seed
1 pound provolone cheese, finely diced (imported recommended)
1 bunch parsley, chopped
1 cup water

Old-Fashioned Scones
Yield, approximately 2 dozen

Preheat oven to 400°.

Sift together flour, baking powder, salt and sugar; cut butter into dry ingredients with pastry knife. Make a well in the mixture, add eggs and milk, stir. Knead in currants until dough is well blended and smooth enough to roll.

Roll out on a lightly floured board to ½-inch thick. Cut into 2-inch biscuits, place on a greased pan. Glaze with egg wash and bake until tops and bottoms are lightly browned, 10 to 12 minutes.

Serve with fresh berry jam and tea.

Old-Fashioned Scones
2 pounds plus 3 ounces all-purpose flour
2 tablespoons plus 1 teaspoon baking powder
1 tablespoon salt
3½ tablespoons sugar
½ pound unsalted butter
4 eggs, beaten
2 cups milk
2 cups currants or raisins
Egg wash glaze (optional):
1 egg mixed with
2 tablespoons water

Mohonk Mountain House

Monterey Hotel

MONTEREY, CALIFORNIA

Designed by local architect W.H. Weeks, the Monterey Hotel was once touted as the Pacific Coast's "daintiest hotel." At its opening in 1904, the *Monterey New Era* wrote, "... the beautiful interior and exterior, the harmonious color effects, the beautifully polished woods, and carpets and furniture chosen with taste and discrimination result in a marvel of luxury and comfort." That description holds true today. Sweeping arches, wrought iron chandeliers and an ornate fireplace grace the main lobby; a flower-filled courtyard and skylit, galleried third-floor lobby lend cheer. Charming rooms sport white-shuttered windows, antique headboards or four-poster beds and colorful coverlets.

Photo, plate 28

Lemon-Blueberry Bread

2 cups flour
¾ cup sugar
½ teaspoon baking powder
1 teaspoon baking soda
1 teaspoon salt
¼ cup lemon pudding mix (dry)
1 egg
1 cup buttermilk
¼ cup lemon curd
2 tablespoons vegetable oil
2 tablespoons sugar
1 cup fresh blueberries

LEMON-BLUEBERRY BREAD

Yield, 1 loaf

In 1602, Spanish explorer Sebastian Vizcaino landed in Monterey and claimed the area for the Spanish crown. At the same site, 162 years later, Captain Gaspar de Portola, accompanied by Father Junipero Serra, ceremoniously founded Mission San Carlos Borromeo. These explorers, along with others, brought with them the seeds of the lemon tree as well as considerable other flora. Many of these plants have since become production crops in California. Lemon, frequently used as a flavoring in baking, is combined here with the blueberry, a Pacific Coast native, to create this delicious breakfast bread.

Preheat oven to 350°.

Mix together flour, sugar, baking powder, soda, salt and pudding mix. In a separate bowl, blend together the egg, buttermilk, lemon curd and oil; stir mixture well into dry ingredients. Sprinkle sugar over blueberries, add to the batter, stirring gently.

Pour into a greased 9 x 5 x 3-inch loaf pan, bake for 50 minutes, or until a pick inserted in the center comes out clean.

California Spinach Dip

Yield, about 4 cups

Thaw spinach and squeeze out excess moisture, mix with balance of ingredients. Serve with your choice of raw sliced vegetables or favorite crackers and chips.

Editor's note: this recipe is nicely presented in a hollowed-out red cabbage.

California Spinach Dip

1 10-ounce package frozen chopped spinach
1 cup mayonnaise
1½ cups sour cream
1 package Knorr's vegetable soup mix
1 8-ounce can water chestnuts, drained and chopped
3 scallions, chopped
Raw sliced vegetables

Apricot Walnut Bread

Yield, 1 loaf

Preheat oven to 325°.

Pour boiling water over butter, apricots and raisins. Sift dry ingredients together and add to the apricot mixture. Add beaten egg and mix well. Add nuts. Pour into a greased loaf pan and bake for 1 hour or until a toothpick inserted into the bread comes out clean.

Editor's note: this is a great recipe for leftover holiday fruits and nuts. Experiment with your favorite dried-fruit and nut combination such as apples and almonds, pineapple and peanuts, etc. (If using salted nuts, decrease salt in recipe accordingly.)

Apricot Walnut Bread

1 cup boiling water
1 tablespoon butter
1 cup diced dried apricots
1 cup raisins
2 cups all-purpose flour
1 cup sugar
1 teaspoon baking powder
1 teaspoon baking soda
½ teaspoon salt
1 egg, beaten
1 cup chopped walnuts

Apple Walnut Salad

Serves 4 to 6

Toss apples with vinegar; add celery, scallions and walnuts. Drizzle with 4 tablespoons walnut oil, toss again. Taste, correct seasoning by adding more vinegar or up to 1 tablespoon walnut oil. Serve immediately.

Apple Walnut Salad

2 Granny Smith apples and
2 Red Delicious apples, cored and chopped (peel on)
½ cup sherry vinegar
1 cup celery, chopped
3 scallions, ½-inch diagonally cut
½ cup shelled walnut halves
4 to 5 tablespoons walnut oil

Monterey Hotel

¾ pound (3 sticks) sweet butter,
 softened
1¾ cups confectioners' sugar
1 egg
2 cups all-purpose flour
1 cup cornstarch
2 cups shelled walnuts, finely
 grated
½ cup red raspberry preserves

LINZER HEARTS
Yield, 4 dozen cookies

Cream butter and 1 cup sugar until light and fluffy, add egg and mix well. Sift together the flour and cornstarch; add to the creamed mixture and blend well. Mix walnuts in thoroughly. Gather dough into a ball, wrap in waxed paper, refrigerate for 4 to 6 hours.

Roll dough out to ¼-inch thick. Using a small heart-shaped cookie cutter, cut out cookies and place on an ungreased cookie sheet. Refrigerate for 45 minutes.

Preheat oven to 325°.

Bake cookies for 10 to 15 minutes, until they are evenly and lightly browned. Remove and cool on rack. While still warm, spread ½ the cookies with raspberry preserves (about ¼ teaspoon jam on each). Top each with 1 of the remaining cookies. Sift the remaining confectioners' sugar and press tops and bottoms of the cookies into the sugar to coat.

The Natchez Eola Hotel

NATCHEZ, MISSISSIPPI

Named "Eola" after the developer's daughter, the seven-story Natchez Eola opened on July 1, 1927, acclaimed as a symbol of civic progress. Beginning in 1932, the hotel was headquarters for the annual Natchez Spring Pilgrimage to local antebellum homes and gardens, and enjoyed years of prosperity and visits by innumerable celebrities. But by the 1960s, the hotel was showing its age, quietly closing in 1974. A detailed restoration brought life back to the dowager, its elaborate chandeliers, marble trim, columns, arched doorways and famed "Peacock Alley" all returned to their original splendor. Once again the embodiment of genteel Southern hospitality, the hotel reopened in 1982.

PEARL STREET PIE
Serves 10 to 12

Pearl Street Pie, appropriately named for the hotel's street, was created by a Natchez resident to cool the taste buds during the hot and humid days of summer. Ice cream has always been relished by Southern natives; the chocolate sauce particularly enhances the flavor of this sweet treat. This fabulous dessert can be enjoyed any season.

Place brownie in bottom of springform cake pan. Spread softened vanilla ice cream on brownie, ½ inch thick; follow with ½ inch layer of coffee ice cream, top with meringue; freeze until firm. Brown meringue under broiler. Top each serving with warmed chocolate sauce.

Photo, plate 29
Pearl Street Pie
Pecan Brownie (page 86)
Vanilla Ice Cream
Coffee Ice Cream
Meringue (page 86)
Chocolate sauce or syrup

Pecan Brownies
½ cup butter
2 tablespoons cocoa
1 cup sugar
2 eggs
½ cup all-purpose flour
1 teaspoon vanilla
1 cup pecans, chopped

Meringue
3 egg whites
¼ teaspoon cream of tartar
6 tablespoons sugar
1 teaspoon vanilla

PECAN BROWNIES
Yield, 9 squares

Preheat oven to 350˚.

Melt butter and cool. Mix cocoa and sugar together. Add eggs, flour and butter, stir until blended. Add vanilla and pecans and mix. Pour into a 9 x 9-inch pan, bake for 30 minutes.

MERINGUE
Yield, tops 1 pie

Beat egg whites and cream of tartar until foamy. Beat in sugar, 1 tablespoon at a time, beating until stiff and glossy. Beat in vanilla.

BLACKENED CATFISH

Yield, 1 large or 2 small servings

Preheat a cast iron skillet until white hot.

Dredge catfish fillet in melted butter, place in skillet skin side down; cook for approximately 3½ to 4 minutes, until edges blacken. Turn fillet, season generously with Cajun spices and cook an additional 3 to 3½ minutes.

Remove to heated serving plate; season with lemon juice, garnish with lemon·slices and parsley.

Blackened Catfish
8 ounces catfish fillets
¼ cup unsalted butter, melted
Cajun spices
Lemon juice
Lemon slices and chopped
  parsley for garnish

SPINACH SALAD

Clean and wash spinach, removing tough stems; place on serving plate.

Sprinkle evenly with mushrooms, chopped eggs, bacon pieces and croutons. Ladle Hot Bacon Dressing over the salad.

Spinach Salad
For each serving:
5 ounces fresh spinach
⅓ cup fresh mushrooms, sliced
1 boiled egg, chopped
5 to 6 tablespoons cooked bacon,
  crumbled
⅓ cup croutons
Hot Bacon Dressing

HOT BACON DRESSING

Yield, approximately 1 cup dressing

Saute bacon until lightly browned, reserve. Add oil (if bacon was too lean) and onion, cooking until onion is tender. Add honey and vinegar and simmer for 5 minutes. Serve hot.

Hot Bacon Dressing
6 to 8 strips bacon, diced
2 tablespoons vegetable oil
¼ cup onion, chopped
¼ cup honey
¼ cup vinegar

The Natchez Eola Hotel

Omni Ambassador East

CHICAGO, ILLINOIS

Chicago, vibrant as any world capital, yet maintaining its flavor as a Midwestern city, is home to the gracious Omni Ambassador East and its world-famous Pump Room. This residentially appointed hotel opened in October, 1926. Its careful renovation is exemplified by the gleaming Italian marble lobby and German crystal chandeliers, capturing the opulent detail of the Gilded Age. The public areas of the hotel and many of the individually decorated guest rooms and suites feature Chinese and English antiques, appointments that have drawn celebrities, public figures and business leaders to this landmark property for more than 60 years.

Photo, plate 30
Roast Breast of Chicken
For each serving:
6 pearl onions
4 tablespoons olive oil
¼ cup water
9 ounces (3 pieces) boneless
  chicken breast, with skin
Salt and cracked black pepper
1 small baked potato, peeled,
  ¼-inch sliced
1 small carrot, peeled, 1-inch
  sliced
3 shiitake mushrooms, halved
1 teaspoon rosemary, chopped
Handful fresh spinach, rinsed
2 tablespoons white wine
1 teaspoon butter

COUNTRY-STYLE ROAST BREAST OF CHICKEN

Ernie Byfield opened The Ambassador East in the 1920s, but it wasn't until 1938 that the Pump Room began to serve guests and celebrities traveling from coast to coast via Chicago, the nation's railroad hub. The Pump Room's Booth Number One became the place to be seen for stars like Judy Garland, Humphrey Bogart, Lauren Bacall and Bette Davis, a tradition that continues today.

Our chefs have always offered flavorful, fresh, simply prepared dishes as well as traditional classics. This free-range chicken dish is a tasty entree prepared with locally grown vegetables and is served in its natural juices.

In small saute pan, saute onions in 2 tablespoons olive oil until golden brown; add 2 tablespoons water, cook until tender, remove from the pan.

Preheat oven to 400°.

Meanwhile, heat 2 tablespoons oil in another pan, add breasts skin-side down. Season with salt and pepper, sear to golden brown. Turn once, add glazed onions and potatoes, carrots, mushrooms and rosemary. Roast in oven for 12 minutes, remove; add spinach and toss. Place chicken and vegetables on serving plate.

To the chicken's saute pan, add white wine and cook over low heat until dry; add ⅓ cup water and bring to a boil. Add butter, stir until melted. Spoon over chicken and serve.

HOME-CURED SALMON GRAVLAX
with Dill Aïoli and Anchovy Toast
Serves 20

Mix salt and sugars together. Pat ½ the mixture on the salmon. Add pepper and dill to the balance, spread on the salmon. Wrap the salmon in plastic and refrigerate for 5 days to cure.

To serve, slice the salmon very thin for the best flavor. Serve accompanied by Dill Aïoli and Anchovy Toast.

Home-Cured Salmon Gravlax
⅓ cup kosher salt
¼ cup light brown sugar
¼ cup granulated sugar
3 pounds (1 side) Atlantic
* salmon, boneless, skin on*
1 tablespoon fresh ground pepper
Small handful fresh dill,
* finely chopped*

DILL AÏOLI
Yield, about ⅔ cup

Preheat oven to 350°.

Arrange peeled garlic and shallots in a shallow baking dish, drizzle with 1 tablespoon olive oil. Cover and bake for 20 minutes, remove from oven, cool.

Blend in balance of ingredients, adding oil slowly. Serve in a small dish next to the salmon.

Dill Aïoli
4 to 5 whole garlic cloves, peeled
1 whole shallot, peeled
½ cup olive oil
1 tablespoon lemon juice
½ teaspoon salt
¼ teaspoon ground pepper
Small handful fresh dill,
* finely chopped*
Pinch saffron
½ cup white wine

ANCHOVY TOAST
Yield, 1 loaf

Preheat oven to 350°.

Thoroughly blend butter, garlic and anchovy paste. Spread on 1 side of the sliced bread. Place on a baking sheet and toast in oven until crisp and slightly browned. Serve in a cloth-lined basket next to the salmon.

Anchovy Toast
1 cup unsweetened butter
1 tablespoon garlic, pureed
¼ cup anchovy paste
1 loaf long French bread,
* sliced ¼-inch thick*

Omni Ambassador East

Pump Room Caesar Salad

For each serving:
2 cups romaine lettuce, cleaned,
  1-inch cut
½ cup garlic salad croutons
4 tablespoons Caesar Dressing
1 anchovy fillet
1 tablespoon fresh parmesan
  cheese, shaved

Caesar Dressing

1 egg yolk
1 teaspoon Dijon mustard
1½ teaspoons garlic, pureed
1½ teaspoons anchovy
  fillets, pureed
1 cup extra virgin olive oil
½ lemon, juiced
1 teaspoon grated parmesan
  cheese

Crème Brûlée

1 cup half-and-half
1 cup heavy cream
½ cup granulated sugar
4 egg yolks
Zest of ½ orange, grated
Sugar, for topping
Fresh raspberries and mint
  leaves, for garnish

PUMP ROOM CAESAR SALAD

Popular since the 20s and 30s, the Caesar salad continues to please those who desire a flavorful, refreshing course either before or after their entree. Today, many Pump Room guests find the Caesar a satisfying alternative to tradition-ally heavier business and social luncheon items.

The secret to an excellent Caesar Salad is the freshness of the romaine lettuce, thoroughly washed and rinsed. Toss together all the ingredients except the anchovy and parmesan, which are used for garnish.

CAESAR DRESSING
Serves 4

Whisk together egg yolk, mustard, garlic and anchovies. Slowly whisk in the olive oil, lemon juice and grated parmesan. Use immediately.

CRÈME BRÛLÉE
Serves 4

Originally a Southern creation, Crème Brûlée has found many enthusiasts seeking a light alternative to creamy desserts for a sweet finish to a meal.

Boil together the creams. In a separate bowl, use a mixer to blend sugar, yolks and zest to a light froth. When cream has boiled, add it to the sugar mixture beating slowly and continuously until smooth.

Preheat oven to 350°.

Divide mixture into individual 6-ounce ramekins; place in water bath and bake for 1 hour, cool. Top each with 2 tablespoons sugar, burn under broiler to a golden brown. Garnish with fresh raspberries and mint.

The Partridge Inn

AUGUSTA, GEORGIA

Area historians note that the excellent cuisine and true warmth and care that Mr. and Mrs. Morris W. Partridge offered guests created their inn's prosperity. The annex for the servants of the Northern and Canadian families who wintered in Augusta is now gone. But hidden somewhere within the inn's walls is the framework of the original 1879 home purchased by Partridge at the turn of the century, which he expanded intermittently over the years to the present five stories and quarter mile of porches and balconies. One of America's few original all-suite hotels, the inn received an award-winning restoration in the mid-1980s, returning it to its original comfort and graciousness.

CRISP DUCK WITH AUGUSTA PEACHES
Serves 10

What could be more Southern-country in flavor than the heartiness of duck and sweetness of fresh peaches ... a synonym for Georgia! This recipe finds its variations in generations of home-cooked meals: roast duck with sauteed spinach and peaches, served with a sauce of honey, lemon, peaches and lime zest.

Preheat oven to 400°.

Roast ducks by seasoning them and placing them breast-side-down in a hot roasting pan. Cook approximately 45 minutes, then turn over and cook for 20 more minutes. Remove from oven and take out breast bone.

To prepare sauce, boil together honey and vinegar to a light syrup, add veal stock and peach juice and adjust seasoning, reduce to thicken; at serving time, quickly blend in the butter.

For each serving, place ½ duck on a bed of blanched spinach, with peaches down the center and the sauce around. Garnish top with blanched lime zest.

Photo, Plate 31
Duck with Augusta Peaches
5 5-pound Long Island ducks
Salt and pepper
½ cup honey
⅓ cup cider vinegar
2 cups veal stock
4½ cups canned Augusta
  peaches, in syrup
¼ cup butter
2 pounds fresh spinach, blanched
Zest of 5 limes, lightly blanched

91

Braised Lamb Shank

10 pounds lamb shank

¾ cup vegetable oil

¼ cup carrots, diced

¼ cup celery, diced

¼ cup onion, chopped

¼ cup leek, sliced

1½ tablespoons garlic, minced

½ cup red wine

4 cups veal stock

1 branch fresh thyme, chopped

½ cup whole garlic cloves, peeled

6 tablespoons tomato paste

1½ pounds fresh spinach

2 pounds potatoes, whipped

BRAISED LAMB SHANK
with whipped potatoes and garlic

Serves 10

Sear lamb shanks in oil in saute pan, transfer to a roasting pan. Preheat oven to 300°.

Saute carrots, celery, onion, leeks and garlic for a few minutes in the same saute pan. Pour sauteed mixture over the shanks, add red wine, veal stock and thyme. Cover roasting pan, bake for 1½ to 2 hours until done to preference. Remove from oven and allow to cool in the juices.

Blanch garlic cloves in boiling water, changing it twice. Prepare sauce by straining pan's liquids; blend in tomato paste, then reduce to thicken. Add blanched garlic cloves and heat through. Meanwhile, blanch spinach in a small amount of boiling water.

Present by spreading blanched spinach on plate, topped with whipped potatoes and lamb shank. Gently nap the plate with sauce, place garlic cloves around the lamb.

She-Crab Soup

¼ cup carrot, chopped

¼ cup celery, chopped

¼ cup leek, chopped

¼ cup onion, chopped

½ cup butter

½ cup all-purpose flour

3 quarts shrimp stock

½ cup heavy cream

2 pounds tomatoes, large-diced

1¼ pounds back-fin crabmeat

*1 bunch spinach, blanched,
 julienne*

1 plum tomato, diced

2 tablespoons parsley, chopped

SHE-CRAB SOUP

Serves 12

Saute carrot, celery, leek and onion in butter until translucent; blend in the flour to make a roux. Add shrimp stock and stir until smooth; incorporate cream. Add diced tomatoes, stew until cooked through, about 15 minutes. Add crab (reserving ½ cup for garnish), heat through.

Garnish bowls with julienne of cooked spinach, diced plum tomato and lump crab, sprinkle top with parsley.

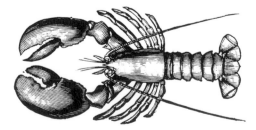

SEAFOOD GUMBO
Serves 12

Prepare roux with oil and flour, cook until just browned. Add vegetables, garlic and herbs, and cool. Dice and cook sausage.

Add chicken stock, diced cooked sausage, Tabasco and Worcestershire, heat through. Mix in shrimp, rice and okra, gently heat to serving temperature.

Seafood Gumbo
⅓ cup vegetable oil
⅓ cup flour
2 red bell peppers, diced
2 green bell peppers, diced
1 cup onion, diced
1 cup celery, diced
2 tablespoons garlic, chopped
1 tablespoon dried thyme
2 bay leaves
Pinch cayenne pepper
½ pound Italian sausage
2½ quarts chicken stock
2 tablespoons Tabasco
⅓ cup Worcestershire
1 pound medium shrimp, cooked
½ cup rice, cooked
1 cup sliced okra, sauteed

PASTA SALAD WITH SHRIMP AND PEPPERS
Serves 10

Cook pasta until done, but still slightly firm to the bite. Peel and devein shrimp, grill or broil to preference. Roast, peel and deseed bell peppers, rough chop. Toss all ingredients together with your favorite vinaigrette dressing.

Pasta Salad with Shrimp and Peppers
30 ounces bow-tie pasta
2 pounds medium shrimp
1 green bell pepper
1 red bell pepper
2 tablespoons parsley, chopped
1 bunch scallions, sliced,
  including part of green tops
⅔ cup vinaigrette dressing

CHOCOLATE BREAD PUDDING
with vanilla sauce
Serves 10

Preheat oven to 300°.

Toast and cube bread.

Create custard by mixing together milk, cream, eggs, sugar and honey. Put toasted bread into individual ramekins, sprinkle with chopped chocolate and roasted hazelnuts, fill each with the custard mixture. Set ramekins in a water bath and bake until custard is set, 45 to 50 minutes.

To serve, pool vanilla sauce on serving plates; loosen puddings and release from ramekins by inverting on the pool of vanilla sauce.

Chocolate Bread Pudding
2 pounds bread
2 cups milk
2 cups heavy cream
8 eggs
½ cup sugar
¼ cup honey
5 ounces bittersweet chocolate,
  chopped
½ cup hazelnuts, roasted
4 cups vanilla sauce

The Partridge Inn

Pinehurst Hotel

PINEHURST, NORTH CAROLINA

Opening New Year's Day, 1901 as "The Carolina," the hotel with its extraordinary polished copper roof and cupola is the centerpiece of the Village of Pinehurst, a National Historic District. Designed by architect Frederick Law Olmsted (who planned New York's Central Park) to duplicate a New England village, Pinehurst was the creation of Boston philanthropist James Walker Tufts, who envisioned a health retreat on the 5,800-acre site. Now an internationally known golf resort, croquet was its original draw; its gun club grew famous under instructor Annie Oakley. The resort's first four golf courses were some of the 400 designed nationally by the legendary architect Donald Ross.

Photo, plate 32

Warm Pumpkin Custard

1 quart heavy cream
¾ cup sugar
1 vanilla bean
8 egg yolks
1 cup pumpkin puree
¼ cup Kentucky bourbon
Brown sugar to glaze
Spiced Peaches (page 95)
Fresh raspberries and mint
* leaves for garnish*

WARM PUMPKIN CUSTARD
with Spiced Richmond County Peaches
Serves 8

Custards have long been an American favorite, dating back to those colonists with English and French roots. The English first boiled custards, later refined by the French into Crème Anglaise and Crème Brûlée. This recipe incorporates the same type of pumpkins used by early North Carolinians in their pies and other desserts.

Preheat oven to 325°.

Warm cream with sugar and vanilla bean to near boiling. Mix egg yolks with pumpkin puree and temper with cream mixture; mix in bourbon. Divide between 8 7-ounce ramekins. Place in water bath and cover.

Bake for approximately 45 minutes until slightly firm on top, but soft in middle. Top with brown sugar and place under broiler until sugar melts.

Place ramekin on a dinner plate. Garnish with fan of Spiced Peaches, raspberries and fresh mint.

SPICED PEACHES
Serves 8

This recipe for Spiced Peaches dates back to colonial times and utilizes fresh Carolina peaches. They are used to prepare many American dishes at the historic Pinehurst Hotel.

Boil together water, schnapps, sugar, cinnamon stick, cloves and lemon juice to create a syrup. Add peaches, gently simmer 8 to 10 minutes until peaches are cooked through. The peaches may be served warm or chilled.

COUNTRY PORK CHOPS
with Cranberry-Pecan Stuffing and Rosemary Mustard Sauce
Serves 8

Boil orange juice to reduce by ¼. Blend orange reduction with basil, tarragon, shallot and orange zest. Whisk in oil slowly. Season with salt and pepper. Cut pocket in pork chops and marinate in the mixture overnight.

Soak cranberries in juice overnight. Drain and place on a cookie sheet with screen racks. Bake in 100° oven slowly until crisp and dried. Reserve ¼ of cranberries for sauce.

Toast whole wheat bread in oven until lightly browned. Place in a mixing bowl along with pecans, cranberries, celery, peppers, onions and sage. Add chicken stock. Mix in butter and eggs by hand. Season with salt and pepper. Stuff pork chops with stuffing, saute in skillet with butter until golden brown.

Place pork chops in 350° oven on roasting pan until done (reserve pan drippings for sauce). Lightly brush top of pork chops with Rosemary Mustard Sauce (page 125) to glaze.

To serve, ladle 2 tablespoons sauce on a dinner plate. Place glazed pork chop in sauce, the bone facing center of the plate. Garnish with toasted cranberries. Place Hopping John (page 96) and Vegetable Bundle (page 96) on the side. Garnish with fresh rosemary sprigs, lightly steamed.

Spiced Peaches
½ cup water
½ cup peach schnapps
¼ cup sugar
1 cinnamon stick
2 whole cloves
2 tablespoons lemon juice
4 fresh ripe peaches, sliced

Country Pork Chops
8 7-ounce rib pork chops, excess fat removed, bones scraped
For marinade, blend:
1 cup fresh orange juice
1 teaspoon fresh basil leaves, chopped
1 teaspoon fresh tarragon leaves, chopped
1 shallot, finely diced
Zest of 1 orange
1 cup olive oil
Salt and fresh ground pepper to taste

Cranberry-Pecan Stuffing
½ cup fresh cranberries
½ cup cranberry juice
3 cups whole wheat bread, crust removed, cubed
¼ cup pecans, chopped
¼ cup celery, finely diced
¼ cup bell pepper, finely diced
¼ cup small onion, finely diced
1 teaspoon sage, chopped
¼ cup chicken stock
2 tablespoons butter, melted
1 egg plus 1 egg white
Salt and pepper to taste

Pinehurst Hotel

Vegetable Bundle

1 large carrot, peeled and
   trimmed
1 large turnip, peeled and
   trimmed
1 rutabaga, peeled and washed
16 heads medium asparagus,
   1½-inch cut
8 plum tomatoes, cut on bias,
   inner flesh removed
Herbed olive oil

VEGETABLE BUNDLE IN PLUM TOMATOES
Serves 8

Wide-cut carrots, turnips and rutabagas. Steam all vegetables lightly, keeping them crisp. Cool.

Preheat oven to 350°.

Place 2 of each vegetable, alternating colors, with plum tomatoes. Brush lightly with herbed olive oil. Bake in a 350° oven until warmed, basting occasionally.

Hopping John

2½ cups blackeyed peas
8 cups ham stock
Dash Tabasco
¼ pound baby collard greens,
   washed, stems removed
2 strips bacon, diced
½ cup Vidalia onion, diced
2½ cups cooked white rice
Salt and ground white pepper
   to taste

HOPPING JOHN
Serves 8

Rinse blackeyed peas in cold water. Place peas and 6 cups ham stock in saucepan. Bring to boil and simmer until tender, but not mushy.

Bring to boil 2 cups ham stock with dash of Tabasco and collards. Simmer till tender adding water when needed. Strain, cool, then dice.

Place bacon in saute skillet. Saute until light brown. Add onions and cook until tender. Add collards. Toss, then remove from heat. Mix with warm rice and blackeyed peas.

Season to taste.

Place mixture in 8 lightly oiled 7-ounce molds or ramekins.

Pack lightly and hold warm for service.

Pinehurst Muffins

4 cups all-purpose flour
2¼ cups sugar
4 teaspoons baking soda
4 teaspoons cinnamon
½ teaspoon salt
4 cups carrots (about 1½
   pounds), grated
1 cup raisins
1 cup pecans, chopped
1 cup coconut, shredded
2 apples, cored, peeled
   and grated
6 eggs, beaten
2 cups vegetable oil
4 teaspoons vanilla extract

PINEHURST MUFFINS
with Vanilla-Honey Butter
Yield, 36 muffins

Preheat oven to 350°.

In a large bowl sift flour, sugar, baking soda, cinnamon and salt. Stir in carrots, raisins, pecans, coconut and apples.

In a bowl, beat eggs and add oil and vanilla. Stir in flour mixture until just combined.

Spoon batter into well-oiled muffin tins. Bake for 15 minutes or until tops of muffins spring back when touched. Let cool 5 minutes, then turn out onto a rack to cool completely. Serve with Vanilla-Honey Butter (page 125).

The Plaza

NEW YORK, NEW YORK

Designed by famed architect Henry Janeway Hardenbergh, "the greatest hotel in the world" opened October 1, 1907. Built on the site of a 15-year-old predecessor by the same name, no expense was spared on the 19-story, French Renaissance "chateau." Marble lobbies, solid mahogany doors, 1,650 crystal chandeliers, Swiss organdy curtains, privately manufactured Irish linens, and gold-incrusted china were just a few of its opulent features. At opening, 90 percent of its guests were permanent residents; overnight guests paid $2.50 per night. Now magnificently restored, The Plaza is honored as a New York City Landmark, a National Historic Landmark, and is in the National Register of Historic Places.

A MOLD OF SWEETBREADS
with Albufera Sauce
Serves 4

A delicate "variety meat" now generally regarded as a gourmet item, sweetbreads were popular in turn-of-the-century America due to their economical cost. Many Europeans coming to this country had fond memories of sweetbreads from their childhood and were delighted to enjoy them again on this side of the Atlantic. The Plaza offers this classic dish, updated for the contemporary palate.

Blanch the sweetbreads, refresh and denerve.

In a deep saucepan, saute the vegetables in butter quickly, then cover with the sweetbreads. Deglaze with a dash of cognac, add veal stock, season with salt and pepper and simmer for 30 to 40 minutes. Allow the sweetbreads to cool in the braising juices. Slice into rondelles and reserve.

Preheat oven to 325°.

For each serving, use a 2-inch high by 3¾-inch round souffle dish. Butter it lightly, line bottom with sweetbread slices. Add a little of the Chicken Mousse and top with a few more slices of the sweetbreads. Bake in a water bath for 20 to 25 minutes. To serve, unmold and place on plates covered with Albufera Sauce. Garnish with chanterelles, vegetables and chervil.

Photo, plate 33
A Mold of Sweetbreads
1 carrot, sliced
1 onion, sliced
2 stalks celery, sliced
3 cloves garlic, chopped
2 tablespoons butter
1 pound fresh sweetbreads
Cognac
1 quart veal stock
Salt and pepper
Chicken Mousse (page 98)
Albufera Sauce (page 98)
Sliced chanterelles and tiny
* root vegetables, steamed, and*
* fresh chervil, for garnish.*

Chicken Mousse

½ pound chicken meat

Salt and pepper

2 slices white bread soaked
  in milk

1½ cups crème fraîche

Chopped truffles and juices
  to taste

Albufera Sauce

½ cup cognac

½ cup madeira

2 cups chicken stock

3 cups heavy cream

Salt and pepper

½ cup duck liver, baked
  and pureed (or use
  commercial foie gras)

Salmon Trout with Red Lettuce

1 3½-pound salmon trout
  (European sea trout or Great
  Lakes steelhead)

12 heads baby red lettuce

Salt and white pepper

½ cup butter or olive oil

Champagne Anise Sauce

2 tablespoons butter

¾ cup shallots, minced

1 stalk celery, rough chopped

1 small carrot, sliced

2 very ripe tomatoes, minced

1 teaspoon tomato paste

1 bottle champagne

4 or 5 star anise (anise fruit)

1 small bouquet garni

Salt and pepper

Butter, for thickening

1 cup heavy cream

Use a food processor to chop chicken meat. Add a seasoning of salt and pepper. Add milk-soaked bread and crème fraîche, blend. Finish with a touch of truffle juice and chopped truffles, reserve.

In a small saucepan, reduce cognac and madeira by ½; add chicken stock, reduce again by ½. Add cream and reduce to a light sauce. Salt and pepper lightly, thicken with liver puree, finish with a touch of truffle juice. Serve very hot.

SALMON TROUT WITH RED LETTUCE
Serves 4

Fresh fillets of salmon trout braised with baby red lettuce in a Champagne and Star Anise sauce ... a very light entree, savory and simple to create.

Fillet the fish, skin carefully and cut in strips, set aside; reserve carcass. Clean and wash lettuce.

In 2 tablespoons butter, lightly saute carcass with the shallots, celery, carrot and tomato until translucent. Add the tomato paste, cook 5 to 10 minutes.

Add champagne and stir; add star anise and bouquet garni, season with salt and pepper. Simmer slowly for about 30 minutes. Strain and reduce by ½, reserving a few tablespoons. Quickly braise the lettuce in the reserved sauce; arrange lettuce on hot serving platter.

Test the sauce for seasoning, adjust; thicken with a bit of butter, reserve.

Salt and pepper fillets and saute in a little olive oil until just pink, arrange on platter. Add cream to sauce, reduce to coating consistency; blend in a bit of butter. Lightly coat the lettuce with the sauce, serve.

Manhattan Style Mussel Chowder

Serves 6 to 8

Scrub the mussels well in several changes of water, scrape off beards, rinse well. Steam the mussels with 1 cup water, covered, over low heat until they are opened (5 to 7 minutes). Use a slotted spoon to transfer mussels to a bowl (discard any that have not opened). Remove mussels from the shells, reserve. Strain the cooking liquid through a cheesecloth-lined sieve, reserve.

In a separate kettle, cook bacon over low heat until crisp, turning frequently. Add onions and bay leaf, cook while stirring until the onion is softened. Add bell pepper and celery, cook about 2 minutes. Add potatoes, tomatoes and juices, mussel liquid, salt and pepper to taste; bring mixture to a boil.

Simmer covered for 25 to 30 minutes, stirring occasionally, until potatoes are tender. Discard bay leaf, add mussels and Tabasco, heat through.

Manhattan Style Mussel Chowder

5 pounds mussels
Water, for steaming
4 slices of lean bacon, diced
½ cup onions, chopped
1 bay leaf
1 cup green bell pepper, chopped
1 cup celery, sliced
1 pound boiling potatoes, peeled, ½-inch diced
28-ounce can (4½ cups) plum tomatoes, drained and chopped
Salt and pepper
Tabasco to taste

Plaza Gingerbread

Yield, 36 to 40 squares

Preheat oven to 350°.

Cream butter, sugar and eggs; stir in molasses and spices. Sift together the flour, baking powder and salt. Add the flour mixture and milk alternately to the butter mixture, beating well after each addition. Add hot water and mix well.

Pour into a greased 13 x 9 x 2-inch baking pan. Bake for 40 to 50 minutes or until a pick inserted in the center comes out clean.

Plaza Gingerbread

1 cup butter, softened
1½ cups light brown sugar
2 eggs, well beaten
¾ cup molasses
1½ teaspoons ground ginger
1½ teaspoons ground nutmeg
1 teaspoon ground cloves
2¾ cups all-purpose flour
1½ teaspoons baking powder
½ teaspoon salt
1 cup milk
¼ cup hot water

The Red Lion Inn

STOCKBRIDGE, MASSACHUSETTS

Established as a stagecoach stop in 1773 and rebuilt in 1897, the Red Lion is one of the few remaining American inns in continuous use since the 18th century. Immortalized in Norman Rockwell's painting *Main Street, Stockbridge,* the inn epitomizes New England hospitality. It is filled with a fine collection of Staffordshire china, colonial pewter and 18th-century furnishings, many of which have belonged to the inn for over a century. Host to five presidents as well as Nathaniel Hawthorne, William Cullen Bryant and Henry Wadsworth Longfellow, The Red Lion is central to Stockbridge's and the Berkshires' historic and cultural attractions.

RED LION LEMON BREAD
Yield, 1 large or 2 small loaves

Photo, plate 34
Red Lion Lemon Bread

1 cup sugar
½ cup butter
2 eggs
Zest of 1 lemon
1½ cups flour
1 teaspoon baking powder
½ teaspoon salt
½ cup nuts, chopped
½ cup milk
For glaze, mix:
Juice of 1 lemon
½ cup sugar

A tradition at The Red Lion Inn. Baked daily in our very own bakery, this lemon bread has healing qualities, brings smiles to those who are blue and satisfies the sweetest tooth! It's sure to welcome all who enter.

Preheat oven to 350°.

Mix ingredients in the order given. Bake in greased loaf pans for 40 to 50 minutes. Spoon glaze over bread while still hot.

AUTUMN BISQUE SOUP

Serves 4 to 6

Add squash, apples, onion, herbs, chicken stock, bread cubes, salt and pepper to a heavy saucepan; bring to a boil and simmer uncovered for 30 to 45 minutes, until squash is softened. Scoop out flesh of squash and discard skins; return pulp to the soup. Use a blender to puree the soup until smooth; return to saucepan.

In a small bowl, beat together egg yolks and cream. Blend a small amount of soup into the egg mixture to temper, then stir the mixture into the saucepan until incorporated. Reheat (do not boil), serve.

Autumn Bisque Soup

1 small butternut squash
  (1 pound), halved and
  seeded, peel remaining
2 green apples, peeled, cored and
  chopped
1 medium onion, chopped
Pinch rosemary
Pinch marjoram
4 cups chicken stock
2 slices white bread, trimmed
  and cubed
1½ teaspoons salt
¼ teaspoon pepper
2 egg yolks
¼ cup heavy cream

SAUTEED SIRLOIN OF VENISON

with mushroom and wine sauce

Serves 2

Flour venison, saute in butter or oil to desired temperature, remove from pan. Add mushrooms, thyme, pepper, saute lightly; add red wine and glace de viande, reduce to a coating consistency; blend in butter. Test for seasonings, salt and pepper if required.

Return venison to pan, reheat; serve topped with sauce.

Sirloin of Venison

1 8- to 10-ounce sirloin
  venison steak
Flour
Butter or oil
½ cup shiitake mushrooms
½ cup oyster mushrooms
Pinch of thyme
Pinch crushed whole black
  peppercorns
¼ cup dry red wine
1 teaspoon glace de viande
1 tablespoon butter
Salt and pepper

The Red Lion Inn

Red Lion Inn Apple Pie
Pie Crust
¼ pound butter, softened
¼ pound vegetable shortening
2¼ cups flour
¾ teaspoon salt
½ cup cold milk
For pie filling:
1 cup granulated sugar
  (extra sugar for top of pie)
1 teaspoon ground cinnamon
10 Macintosh apples, peeled,
  cored, sliced
1 tablespoon butter
Egg wash (1 egg whisked
  with 1 tablespoon milk)

Cold Strawberry Soup
3¼ pounds frozen sliced
  or pureed strawberries
½ teaspoon cinnamon
½ teaspoon salt
1 cup frozen orange juice
  concentrate
1 cup water
¼ cup burgundy wine
5 cloves
3 tablespoons cornstarch
2½ pounds vanilla ice cream
1 quart light cream
Strawberries, for garnish

Indian Pudding
4 cups milk
4 tablespoons butter
½ cup cornmeal
½ cup molasses
¼ cup sugar
1 cup apples, chopped
½ cup raisins
½ teaspoon cinnamon
1½ teaspoon ginger
½ teaspoon salt
1 egg

RED LION INN APPLE PIE
Yield, 1 double-crust pie

Blend together butter and shortening. Mix together flour and salt, and cut in butter/shortening blend. Add milk and mix quickly. Divide into 2 equal portions, roll out into crusts.

Preheat oven to 375°.

Combine sugar and cinnamon, and add to sliced apples until well mixed.

Fill pie shell with filling and dot with butter. Cover with top crust. Brush top crust with egg wash. Sprinkle with granulated sugar. Pierce top crust. Bake for approximately 1 hour or until apples are tender when tested with a thin knife.

COLD STRAWBERRY SOUP
Serves 10 to 12

Mix first 7 ingredients, bring to a boil; blend in cornstarch, cook until thickened. Cool to room temperature, remove cloves. Add ice cream and light cream, stir until blended. Refrigerate for 1 hour. Garnish each serving with fresh strawberries.

INDIAN PUDDING
Serves 8 to 10

Combine 2½ cups milk with butter and scald. Combine ½ cup milk and cornmeal, add to scalded milk and butter. Cook 20 minutes, stirring slowly so mixture does not burn. Add molasses, sugar, apples and raisins. Stir in cinnamon, ginger, salt and egg. Cook 5 more minutes.

Preheat oven to 325°.

Pour mixture into a well-greased shallow pan. Pour remaining cup of milk over this. Bake for 1½ hours or until pudding is set.

Serve warm with ice cream and/or whipped cream.

St. James Hotel

RED WING, MINNESOTA

Nestled between limestone bluffs on the banks of the Mississippi River, Red Wing was the world's largest primary wheat market in the early 1870s. In 1875, local businessmen built the St. James in celebration of the city's prosperity. Operated by the Lillyblad family for 72 years, its restaurant was renowned. Trains would regularly stop so that passengers could enjoy dining at "Clara's." Purchased by the Red Wing Shoe Company, the Italianate hotel enjoyed a detailed restoration, completed in 1979. Each of the guest rooms is named for a 19th-century riverboat and is individually decorated in Victorian antiques and reproductions, including handmade quilts and period wallcoverings.

CLARA'S BREAD PUDDING
with Brandy Sauce
Serves 6 to 8

In the early 1870s, Red Wing became the largest primary wheat market in the world. The St. James Hotel was built to accommodate the many travelers to Red Wing. The hotel was a smashing success under the direction of the Lillyblad family; Clara Lillyblad became a local legend through her charm and hospitality.

Clara's Bread Pudding with Brandy Sauce has been one of the, if not the, most popular items at the St. James Hotel through the years.

Preheat oven to 350°.

Mix eggs, milk, sugar, vanilla and seasonings. Blend well with bread products. Pour into a well-greased 9 x 9-inch cake pan and bake for 45 to 60 minutes. Top each 3 x 3-inch serving with Brandy Sauce.

ST. JAMES' BRANDY SAUCE

Beat eggs until they are light in color. Add eggs slowly to the sugar and set aside. Whip cream, add brandy to the whipped cream; fold in egg and sugar mixture. Mix well, refrigerate.

Photo, plate 35

Clara's Bread Pudding
10 large eggs, mixed slightly
1 pint milk or half-and-half
1 cup granulated sugar*
½ tablespoon vanilla extract
½ tablespoon ground cinnamon
⅛ teaspoon ground nutmeg
⅛ teaspoon ground allspice
1 quart leftover cinnamon
* or sweet rolls, finely diced*
1 quart French-style bread,
* finely diced*
*More sugar may be necessary if
* leftover cinnamon/sweet rolls*
* are unavailable and additional*
* bread must be used.*

Brandy Sauce
2 eggs
1 cup confectioners' sugar
1 cup whipping cream
¼ cup brandy, or to taste

Sheraton Moana Surfrider

HONOLULU, HAWAII

Highlighted by a three-story, Ionic-columned porte cochere, two colonnaded verandas, intricate millwork, coffered ceilings, and furnishings of a different fine wood on each floor, the original 75-room Moana, Waikiki's first hotel, opened in 1901. The 1918 addition of two Italianate wings began the hotel's expansion and created the Banyan Court, home to the famed *Hawaii Calls* radio broadcast for 40 years. An historic banyan tree, planted in 1885, is the focal point of this oceanfront venue, the teak-floored Banyan Veranda opening onto the court and the Pacific Ocean beyond. An exacting 20-month, $50 million restoration has confirmed the Moana's position as "The First Lady of Waikiki."

Photo, plate 36

Eggs Volga

4 eggs

4 slices fine-cured ham, thinly sliced

4 slices light rye bread

4 1-ounce artichoke bottoms

1 ounce beluga caviar

Fresh herbs of your choice, for garnish

Salt and pepper to taste

Champagne Sauce

Yield, approximately 1½ cups

1 tablespoon shallots, finely chopped

1 tablespoon white wine vinegar

4 egg yolks

1 cup clarified butter

⅓ cup fine champagne

1 tablespoon fresh tarragon leaves, finely chopped

Salt and pepper to taste

TURN-OF-THE-CENTURY EGGS VOLGA
with Champagne Sauce
Serves 4

The "Gay 90s": steamships made the exotic Hawaiian Islands available to visitors, and, accordingly, the elegant Moana opened to accommodate them comfortably. Anything with a European flavor, and particularly the grandiose flavor of mysterious, far-off Russia, was in vogue. This simple yet elegant dish—especially appropriate for a friendly brunch—honors not only the universal celebrant, champagne, but the most exquisite of imported Russian flavors, caviar.

Poach eggs for 3 minutes. Fry both sides of ham lightly in a buttered skillet. Trim crust from rye bread allowing a 4-inch square, toast. Braise artichoke bottoms in the buttered skillet.

Place rye toast on plate. In order, top with an artichoke bottom, slice of ham (nicely folded) and poached egg. Top with Champagne Sauce and ¼ ounce of caviar. Garnish with fresh herbs. Season to taste.

For sauce, bring shallots and vinegar to boil in small saucepan, reducing slowly until almost dry; cool to lukewarm.

Add egg yolks, beating with whisk gently until light yellow. Slowly incorporate butter, then champagne. Keep warm.

At serving time add tarragon leaves, salt and pepper to taste.

VEAL MEDALLIONS WITH TRUFFLES

on madeira sauce

Gently press chopped truffles on top of veal. Saute bottom of the cut in butter, then turn and saute truffle-breaded face; remove from pan, keep warm.

Remove excess fat from pan, deglaze with a splash of madeira; add veal glaze, reduce slightly. Add ice-cold butter to sauce; salt and pepper to taste.

Quickly saute vegetables in butter.

To serve, pour sauce onto serving plate, arrange veal medallions and vegetables on the sauce.

Veal Medallions
For each serving:
1½ tablespoons truffles, chopped
2 2½-ounce veal tenderloin medallions
1 tablespoon butter
Madeira wine
3 tablespoons veal glaze
1 tablespoon butter, iced
Salt and pepper to taste
For vegetables:
1 tablespoon butter
4 baby carrots
2 baby yellow squash
2 baby green squash

SAUTEED SCALLOPS AND KAHUKU PRAWNS

on Beetroot Sauce

Saute scallops (until just firm) and prawns in butter until cooked (prawns are done when they just turn opaque and lose translucency).

Pour Beetroot Sauce onto serving plate, arranging sauteed scallops and prawns on top. Add sauteed snow peas to center, top with boiled potatoes.

Scallops and Kahuku Prawns
For each serving:
3 scallops
3 Kahuku prawns*
  (Hawaiian freshwater prawns), shells removed
2 tablespoons butter
*Should you be unable to acquire prawns, large fresh shrimp are an acceptable substitute.
For vegetables:
1 ounce snow peas, julienne, lightly sauteed
2 small potatoes, boiled

BEETROOT SAUCE

Yield, approximately ½ cup

Saute shallots and beetroot briefly in butter. Deglaze with a splash of sherry vinegar and fish stock, continue cooking until beetroot is tender. Liquidize in a blender; return to pan, add cream and reduce. Finish with ice-cold butter, salt and pepper to taste.

Beetroot Sauce
1½ tablespoons shallots, chopped
3 tablespoons beetroot, diced
1½ tablespoons butter
Sherry vinegar
3 tablespoons fish stock
¼ cup heavy cream
1½ tablespoons butter, iced
Salt and pepper

Sheraton Moana Surfrider

Poached Onaga on Spinach
For each serving:
*1 7-ounce onaga (Hawaiian
  snapper), skin on, cleaned*
¼ pound spinach leaves
1 teaspoon butter
2 new potatoes, boiled
For garnish:
*Tomato puree, fennel sprigs, and
  1½ tablespoons fennel, diced*

Saffron Sauce
For each serving:
*1 scant tablespoon shallots,
  finely chopped*
1½ tablespoons fennel, diced
1½ tablespoons butter
1 tablespoon white wine
1 tablespoon pernod
3 tablespoons fish stock
*A few pistils saffron or pinch
  saffron powder*
¼ cup heavy cream
Salt and pepper to taste

Spinach Salad with Duck
For each serving:
*1½ tablespoons Balsamic
  Vinaigrette*
3½ ounces spinach, cleaned
*1½ ounces button mushrooms,
  sliced*
*1½ ounces smoked duck breast
  (skin removed), thinly sliced*
Balsamic Vinaigrette
Yield, ½ cup
Blend:
3 tablespoons balsamic vinegar
3 tablespoons vegetable oil
3 tablespoons olive oil
1 tablespoon shallots, chopped
1 tablespoon sun-dried tomatoes
1 teaspoon basil, chopped
Salt and pepper to taste

POACHED ONAGA ON SPINACH
with Saffron Sauce

Poach onaga in 1 inch of boiling water until fork tender, 10 to 15 minutes. Saute spinach in butter until wilted, place in center of serving plate. Place onaga on top of spinach, surround with Saffron Sauce. Place boiled potatoes on the plate, garnish with tomato puree and fennel.

SAFFRON SAUCE

Saute shallots and fennel in ½ of the butter. Deglaze pan with wine, reduce. Add pernod, fish stock and saffron and cream, reduce sauce to coating consistency. Stir in balance of butter, salt and pepper to taste.

SPINACH SALAD WITH SMOKED DUCK BREAST
and Balsamic Vinaigrette

Add vinaigrette to a large bowl. Add spinach leaves, toss until well coated. Remove to serving plate, top with mushrooms and duck breast.

Photography: Kanji Takeno

COLOR PLATE 25
Poached Shrimp and Scallops with Asparagus, page 73
The Mayflower — A Stouffer Hotel, Washington, D.C.

Photography: Al Rendon

COLOR PLATE 26
Menger Grilled Chicken Salad, page 76
Menger Hotel, San Antonio, Texas

Photography: Dick Busher

COLOR PLATE 27
Breakfast on the Balcony, page 79
Mohonk Mountain House, New Paltz, New York

Photography: Patrick Tregenza

COLOR PLATE 28
Lemon-Blueberry Bread, page 82
Monterey Hotel, Monterey, California

Photography: Mark Coffey

COLOR PLATE 29
Pearl Street Pie, page 85
The Natchez Eola Hotel, Natchez, Mississippi

Photography: Steinkamp/Ballogg

COLOR PLATE 30
Country-Style Roast Breast of Chicken, page 88
Omni Ambassador East, Chicago, Illinois

COLOR PLATE 31
Crisp Duck with Augusta Peaches, page 91
The Partridge Inn, Augusta, Georgia

Photography: Frank Pierce

COLOR PLATE 32
Warm Pumpkin Custard, page 94
Pinehurst Hotel, Pinehurst, North Carolina

Stouffer Tower City Plaza Hotel

CLEVELAND, OHIO

In 1815, Cleveland's first hotel, Mowrey's Tavern, opened on the site of today's Stouffer Tower City Plaza Hotel. Built as part of a master plan for a downtown railroad terminal, the original 1,000-room property opened December 16, 1918, boasting a 10-story atrium at its core. A white brick, neoclassical building, the hotel was designed in an "E" shape to allow maximum natural lighting in all rooms. Excellent craftsmanship distinguishes the hotel: the facade is embellished with multiple cast-stone details, balustrades, ornamentation and bronze canopies. An ambitious $37-million renovation has returned the hotel to its original grandeur.

SAUTEED VEAL CHOPS
with Braised Endives and Passion Fruit Sauce
Serves 4

Dining at Cleveland's landmark hotel has long been a tradition of elegance and culinary imagination. Chef Necip Erturk, executive chef of Stouffer Tower City Plaza Hotel, is internationally known for his innovative presentation and creative interpretations of classic cuisine, including this delicately prepared veal chop entree.

For endives: place onion and endives in a small casserole, season with salt and pepper, sugar and lemon juice. Add chicken stock and butter, bring to a boil and cover. Braise in oven until tender, 20 to 25 minutes. Drain endives and separate heads. Brown in clarified butter, 1 minute on each side.

For sauce: in a small pan lightly saute chopped shallots in clarified butter. Deglaze with wine until almost dry. Add demi-glace and passion fruit puree. Bring to a boil and fold in butter, strain.

Preheat oven to 350°.

Salt and pepper whole shiitakes, brush with butter and grill ½ minute on each side. Lightly brown shallots in 1 tablespoon butter seasoned with salt and pepper. Braise in oven until tender, 5 to 10 minutes.

To serve: saute chops in clarified butter over medium heat until done to preference, season to taste. Place chop on a plate covered with Passion Fruit Sauce and surround with Braised Endives and mushroom garniture.

Photo, plate 37

Braised Endives
½ medium onion, sliced
4 medium Belgian endives, whole
Salt and pepper
¼ teaspoon sugar
2 drops lemon juice
½ cup chicken stock or water
1 tablespoon butter
2 tablespoons clarified butter

Passion Fruit Sauce
½ tablespoon shallots, chopped
1 tablespoon clarified butter
¼ cup white wine
½ cup veal demi-glace
⅓ cup passion fruit puree
½ tablespoon butter
Mushroom garniture:
Salt and pepper
16 shiitake mushrooms, de-stemmed
Butter
8 shallots, peeled

Veal Chops
4 10-ounce center-cut veal chops
4 tablespoons clarified butter
Salt and pepper

Marinade
½ teaspoon coarse-cracked
  peppercorns
½ tablespoon juniper berries
1 tablespoon brandy
2 tablespoons vegetable oil
Beet Timbale
½ cup beet puree
5 egg yolks
1 cup heavy cream
Salt and pepper to taste
Beet Anna
2 fresh medium beets, peeled
  and thinly sliced
Salt and pepper to taste
3 tablespoons clarified butter
Venison Sauce
½ tablespoon shallots, chopped
1 teaspoon black peppercorns
10 juniper berries
1 tablespoon clarified butter
2 tablespoons brandy
¼ cup beet juice
¾ cup venison demi-glace
1 tablespoon butter
8 3-ounce venison loin
  medallions
Clarified butter

MEDALLION OF WHITE TAIL VENISON
with Beet Anna and Beet Timbale
Serves 4

Make marinade of peppercorns, juniper berries, brandy and vegetable oil, add venison, marinate 1 hour.

Preheat oven to 350°.

For Timbale: whisk beet puree, egg yolks and heavy cream until blended, season with salt and pepper. Place in greased 4 x 2½ x 3-inch diameter mold. Bake in a water bath until firm, 10 to 15 minutes.

Preheat oven to 350°.

For Beet Anna: towel-dry beet slices, season with salt and pepper, toss with clarified butter. Layer in a 3-inch circle, overlapping beets by ½. Bake 3 to 4 minutes.

For sauce: saute shallots, peppercorns and juniper berries in clarified butter for 2 to 3 minutes. Deglaze the pan with brandy, add beet juice and reduce until almost dry. Add venison demi-glace and bring to a boil, fold in butter, strain.

To serve: saute venison to medium rare in heated clarified butter (3 to 4 minutes per side). Pour Venison Sauce on serving plates, top with 2 medallions per serving. Garnish with Beet Anna and Beet Timbale.

Whole Lobster-Tail Salad
4 1¼-pound lobsters, boiled
Melon-Cucumber Confetti
½ cantaloupe
1 cucumber, peeled
½ red bell pepper, peeled
  and diced
1 teaspoon fresh dill leaves
1 tablespoon lime juice
2 tablespoons olive oil
Salt and pepper to taste

WHOLE LOBSTER-TAIL SALAD
with Melon-Cucumber Confetti
Serves 4

Break each lobster tail from the body, reserve claws. Remove tail shells, allowing tail fin to remain intact. Split tail in half to about 2 inches from the fin.

Scoop out cantaloupe and cucumber in small ovals. Toss with balance of ingredients, salt and pepper to taste, toss lightly.

Place each tail on its serving plate in a decorative "V" shape. Arrange Melon-Cucumber Confetti within the "V". Crack claws and arrange on either side.

FLOURLESS CHOCOLATE CAKE
with Sauce Anglaise
Yield, 1 10-inch cake

Lightly brush with butter (or spray with nonstick coating) the bottom and sides of cake pan, line with paper.

Preheat oven to 350°.

Beat egg yolks with ½ cup sugar until thick and fluffy. Beat egg whites with cream of tartar and ½ cup sugar until light and fluffy. Mix butter with warm chocolate until dissolved and smooth; fold in the egg yolk mixture, then the egg whites, pour into prepared pan. Bake for 35 to 40 minutes, until firm.

Remove from oven, cool for 15 minutes, then separate cake from pan by running a small spatula around the edge; remove the paper from the cake's sides. Allow to cool for 45 minutes, turn cake upside down and re-move paper from bottom. Refrigerate until ready to serve.

To serve, dust the top of the cake with confectioners' sugar, decorate the side of each plate with Sauce Anglaise.

For Sauce: boil milk. Whip egg yolks and sugar until fluffy. Pour the milk over the egg mixture and place over a hot water bath; whisk the mixture until thick. Remove from heat, mix for 1 minute, allow to cool. A few tablespoons (or to taste) of flavored liqueurs may be added to flavor the Sauce Anglaise.

Flourless Chocolate Cake
8 egg yolks
1 cup sugar
5 egg whites
Pinch cream of tartar
1 cup butter, unmelted
8 ounces bittersweet chocolate,
  melted, left slightly warm
Sauce Anglaise
2 cups milk
4 egg yolks
1 cup sugar

Stouffer Tower City Plaza Hotel

The Tutwiler—A Camberley Hotel

BIRMINGHAM, ALABAMA

For 60 years after its 1914 opening, the Tutwiler was *the* gathering place for Alabama's business circles, until being frazed by implosion in 1974. Recreated through the renovation of one of Birmingham's oldest and most prominent addresses—the Ridgely Apartment Building—the new Tutwiler opened in 1986. Built and financed by Edward Magruder Tutwiler in 1913, the Ridgely's exceptional Italianate architectural details provide an ambience for today's Tutwiler equal to that of its predecessor. Elegantly furnished with turn-of-the-century antiques and reproductions, the hotel houses a unique collection of art including paintings on loan from the city's Museum of the Arts.

ROAST SQUAB AU CRESSON
with Currant Butter and Salad Birmingham
Serves 4

This recipe was inspired by the menu served to the guests invited to celebrate the Grand Opening of the original Tutwiler Hotel, on June 15, 1914. This was the salad course served near the end of the buffet muscovite. Other selections from the menu read as follows: Hot or Cold Tomato Broth, Chicken Camelia, Crudite of Nuts and Pickled Items, Aiguillette of Pompano, Walewska, Potatoes Hollandaise, Filet Mignon Bouquetiere, Asparagus Sauce Mousseline, Sherbet Creme de Menthe, Fancy Ice Cream and Assorted Cakes, Cheese and Crackers, and Demi Tasse. The price for the Table d'Hote was $3.00.

Remove the backbones from the squab; make a small slit in the excess skin at the bottom end of the breast; insert drumsticks, fold back wings.

Make marinade for squab using olive oil, rosemary, garlic, lemon juice and soy sauce; marinate 1 hour. Grill squab for approximately 5 minutes per side, until breasts are firm to the touch, set aside.

Mix butter, reduced amaretto and currants with mixer, set aside.

Mix orange juice and zest with seasoning mix, whisk in olive oil; add watercress and salad leaves, toss, place on plates. Place squab in center of plate and top with Currant Butter, garnish with orange zest.

Photo, plate 38

Roast Squab

4 squab
½ cup olive oil
2 small bunches rosemary
1 clove garlic, minced
Juice of 1 lemon
⅛ cup soy sauce

Currant Butter

¼ pound butter, softened
½ cup amaretto reduced until alcohol is removed
2 cups currants

Salad Birmingham

Juice and zest of 1 orange
Seasoning mix (equal parts granulated garlic, granulated onion and white pepper)
4 tablespoons olive oil
2 bunches watercress
2 heads hydroponically grown bibb lettuce
2 heads baby red oak leaf lettuce
1 head radicchio

ROASTED RABBIT SALAD

Serves 6 to 8

Preheat oven to 350°.

Rub rabbits with salt and pepper, place on pan. Roast for 15 to 20 minutes or until done. Let cool, bone rabbit, dice meat into large chunks. Place in a bowl, mix in celery, pomegranate, raisins, pine nuts and truffles, add olive oil and balsamic vinegar. Season with cardamon, coriander and seasoning mix.

Roasted Rabbit Salad
2 2½- to 3-pound whole rabbits
Salt and pepper to taste
1 cup celery, diced
1 pomegranate
1 cup raisins, marinated in warm amaretto
½ cup pine nuts
1 small truffle, julienne
½ cup olive oil
¼ cup balsamic vinegar
Cardamon
Coriander
Seasoning mix (1 part granulated garlic, 1 part granulated onion, 1 part white pepper)

GOAT CHEESE FRITTERS

with grits and honey mustard

Serves 4 to 6

Combine grits, salt and butter. Add boiling milk. Add egg yolks, goat cheese, honey, mustard and salt. Stir well.

Roll up in parchment paper to 2-inch-thick roll. Chill.

Cut into medallions and dip into flour, egg wash and breadcrumbs. Pan fry in butter.

Goat Cheese Fritters
1 cup hominy grits
⅛ teaspoon salt
1 tablespoon butter
½ cup milk, heated to boiling
2 egg yolks
2 ounces goat cheese
⅛ cup pure honey
1 tablespoon dry English mustard
Salt
Flour for dredging
1 egg, beaten, for egg wash
Breadcrumbs for coating
Butter for frying

The Tutwiler

Cream of Pumpkin Soup

1 pie pumpkin

¼ cup amaretto

1 cup chicken stock

2 cups heavy cream

¼ to ½ cup light brown sugar

*Mace, cinnamon and nutmeg
  to taste*

CREAM OF PUMPKIN SOUP
Serves 4 to 6

Preheat oven to 325°.

Puncture the pumpkin with a paring knife in 5 or 6 places around the pumpkin. Place on a baking sheet and roast for 35 to 45 minutes until it becomes dark brown. Cool pumpkin in ice water, remove seeds and the skin. Puree pulp in a food processor.

In a 4-quart saucepan, over medium heat, blend the amaretto and chicken stock; reduce by half, add pumpkin puree. Bring to a boil, add cream; stir in brown sugar, mace, cinnamon and nutmeg. Adjust seasoning to slightly sweet with brown sugar (depending on the saltiness of the chicken stock).

White Chocolate Brownies

1 cup butter

*1 pound white chocolate,
  coarsely chopped*

2 eggs

Pinch salt

1 cup sugar

1 teaspoon vanilla

1 teaspoon salt

2 cups all-purpose flour

*1 pound semi-sweet chocolate
  chips*

WHITE CHOCOLATE BROWNIES
Yield, 32 squares

Preheat oven to 350°.

Cut parchment to fit 2 8x8x2-inch pans and spray with non-stick coating. Melt butter and reserve. Add ½ of white chocolate mixture; do not stir.

Beat eggs with pinch of salt till frothy. Gradually add sugar and beat until pale yellow (slowly dissolving ribbons should form when beaters are lifted). Add butter, remaining white chocolate mixture, vanilla, salt and flour. Mix just till combined. Stir in semi-sweet chocolate chips and remaining white chocolate chips.

Place in prepared pans. Smooth top. Bake approximately 20 minutes (cover top with foil if they seem to be browning too quickly).

The Wauwinet

The Wauwinet, constructed with a typical Nantucket wood-shingle facade in the mid 19th century, opened as a restaurant serving "shore dinners." Guests usually arrived by boat. The first guest rooms were incorporated in 1876. Totally refurbished in 1988 at a cost of $3 million, accommodations feature individual design schemes of chintz, polished brass, scrimshaw and Audubon prints. Trompe l'oeil finishes and floor coverings add whimsical charm. Situated at the base of the Great Point Nature Preserve, with over 20 miles of unspoiled shoreline, The Wauwinet is surrounded by the white-sand beaches of Nantucket Bay to the west and the Atlantic Ocean to the east.

NANTUCKET SMOKED SEAFOOD CHOWDER
Serves 6 to 8

A century ago, guests would take the Miss Lillian, *a catboat, up the head of the harbor to Wauwinet for a "shore meal" served outside. The hotel replicated this historical service in 1990.*

Guests now board the Anna W II *in town for a 1-hour cruise up harbor to* TOPPER'S, *the inn's restaurant. Arriving at The Wauwinet about 6:30 P.M., they sit on the deck, silhouetted in the sunset, watching the chefs prepare a traditional shore meal.*

This delightful chowder, the first item served at TOPPER'S *shore meal, uses select smoked seafood products—scallops, bluefish, yellowfin tuna and mussels—all from Nantucket waters.*

Melt butter, add flour to make roux; cook 5 minutes, reserve.

Render salt pork, reserving fat; discard salt pork. Saute onions in fat until clear; add celery, bay leaves and thyme, cook 3 minutes. Add chicken stock and clam juice, bring to a boil, cook for 20 minutes.

Add potatoes, boil for 10 minutes. Add all smoked seafood and boil for 10 to 15 minutes.

Add roux by spoonfuls (allowing mixture to cook between additions) until thickened; cook 5 minutes. Add sherry, hot sauce, salt and white pepper. Add cream and let boil until it reaches desired consistency.

Photo, plate 39
Smoked Seafood Chowder
¼ pound butter
¾ cup flour
6 ounces salt pork, diced
1 large onion, diced
3 stalks celery, diced
2 bay leaves
½ teaspoon dried or
 fresh thyme, chopped
1 quart chicken stock
2 cups clam juice
2 large potatoes, diced
½ pound smoked Nantucket Bay
 scallops
½ pound smoked bluefish
¼ pound smoked yellowfin tuna
¼ pound smoked mussels
4 tablespoons sherry
2 shakes hot sauce
Kosher salt to taste
White pepper to taste
2 cups heavy cream
Nantucket Clam Chowder
*If you do not like smoked
 products, fresh chopped
 clams may be substituted
 for Nantucket Clam Chowder.*

Wauwinet Lamb Sandwich
Grilled Lamb

4 large cloves garlic

2 large shallots

1 cup olive oil

1/3 cup red wine vinegar

4 fresh rosemary sprigs or
* 1 tablespoon dried, crumbled*

4 fresh thyme sprigs or 2
* teaspoons dried, crumbled*

1 long strip orange peel
* (zest portion only)*

1 long strip lemon peel
* (zest portion only)*

1 tablespoon coarse
* cracked pepper*

1 1¼-pound piece boneless leg of
* lamb, butterflied, scored and*
* trimmed of fat*

Coarse salt

For the sandwiches:

4 6-inch baguettes, halved
* lengthwise*

Olive oil, for brushing

Onion Marmalade (page 115)

½ head curly endive

Grilled Lamb

Fried Eggplant

Fried Eggplant

1 cup flour

1 cup bread crumbs

2 eggs

1 eggplant, peeled and
* sliced lengthwise*

2 tablespoons olive oil

WAUWINET LAMB SANDWICH

Grilled Lamb Sandwich with Fried Eggplant and Onion Marmalade …
this is TOPPER'S *restaurant's most popular sandwich.*

Serves 4

With food processor running, drop garlic and shallots through feed tube, process until minced. Transfer contents to a heavy, large, self-sealing plastic bag. Add oil, vinegar, herbs, peels and pepper; add lamb, toss to coat well. Seal, refrigerate 12 to 24 hours, turning bag occasionally.

Preheat grill to very hot. Remove lamb from marinade, sprinkle with salt. Sear lamb on grill until slightly crusty-charred, then cook slowly until medium rare, about 15 minutes. Cool to room temperature, slice thin.

Brush split baguette with olive oil and grill until slightly charred and crusty. Spread bottom half with ¼ cup Onion Marmalade (page 115). Top with endive, Grilled Lamb and Fried Eggplant.

Cut in half and serve.

FRIED EGGPLANT

4 servings

Place flour and bread crumbs in separate pans. Lightly beat eggs in a bowl large enough to accommodate the eggplant. Dredge eggplant in flour, then egg and bread crumbs. Fry eggplant in olive oil until golden brown.

Editor's note: fried eggplant also makes a delicious vegetable dish when served with a sprinkling of grated parmesan cheese and fresh ground black pepper.

Photography: Claude Rolo

COLOR PLATE 33
A Mold of Sweetbreads with Albufera Sauce, page 97
The Plaza, New York, New York

Photography: Lincoln Russell

COLOR PLATE 34
Red Lion Lemon Bread, page 100
The Red Lion Inn, Stockbridge, Massachusetts

Photography: Ken LeGros

COLOR PLATE 35
Clara's Bread Pudding, page 103
St. James Hotel, Red Wing, Minnesota

Photography: David Franzen

COLOR PLATE 36
Turn-of-the-Century Eggs Volga, page 104
Sheraton Moana Surfrider, Honolulu, Hawaii

Beth Segal Photography

COLOR PLATE 37
Veal Chops with Endive and Passion Fruit Sauce, page 107
Stouffer Tower City Plaza Hotel, Cleveland, Ohio

Photography: Southern Living Magazine

COLOR PLATE 38
Roast Squab au Cresson, page 110
The Tutwiler — A Camberley Hotel, Birmingham, Alabama